Pathways

Textured Knits Collection
by Knit Picks

Photography by John Cranford
Graphic Design by Lee Meredith

Printed in the United States of America
First Printing, 2020

ISBN 978-1-62767-304-4

Versa Press, Inc.

800-447-7829
www.versapress.com

CONTENTS

ABINGDON PULLOVER

by Donna Estin

FINISHED MEASUREMENTS

39.5 (44.25, 48.75, 51.75)(56.5, 59.5, 64, 68.5)" finished bust circumference; meant to be worn with 10" positive ease
Sample is 44.25" size; model is 33.5" bust

YARN

Paragon™ (sport weight, 50% Fine Merino Wool, 25% Baby Alpaca, 25% Mulberry Silk; 123 yards/50g): Pimento 26970, 11 (12, 13, 14)(15, 17, 18, 19) balls

NEEDLES

US 5 (3.75mm) straight or circular needles (24" or longer), or size to obtain gauge

US 4 (3.5mm) 16" circular needles, or one size smaller than size used to obtain gauge

NOTIONS

Yarn Needle
Stitch Markers
Stitch Holders or Scrap Yarn

GAUGE

23 sts and 34 rows = 4" in Beaded Rib on larger needles, blocked
21 sts and 34 rows = 4" in Barter Stitch on larger needles, blocked

For pattern support, contact donnaestindesigns@gmail.com

Abingdon Pullover

Notes:

Texture that looks intricate but is easy to create is the cornerstone of the Abingdon Pullover. This loose-fitting, boxy pullover uses a deeply textured, elegant ribbing on the hem and cuffs, then transitions to an allover simple texture on the body and sleeves.

Drop shoulder sleeves are kept trim through the upper arm for a modern look. Pullover is worked flat from the bottom up and seamed. The neckline begins with just enough 1x1 Rib to hold it in place, then is finished with a stockinette rolled neckline.

Measure lengths vertically with weight of piece hanging from needles or by counting rows.

Yarn with drape will have fewer rows per inch on a full garment than a 4″ square swatch. When in doubt, stop 2″ before pattern's stated length, wet block, then work additional rows after piece dries if needed.

Charts are worked flat; read RS rows (odd numbers) from right to left, and WS rows (even numbers) from left to right.

Beaded Rib (flat over a multiple of 5 sts plus 2)
Row 1 (RS): P2, (K1, P1, K1, P2) to end.
Row 2 (WS): (K2, P3) to last 2 sts, K2.
Rep Rows 1–2 for pattern.

Barter (flat over a multiple of 4 sts)
Row 1 (RS): K across.
Row 2 (WS): (K2, P2) to end.
Row 3: K across.
Row 4: (P2, K2) to end.
Rep Rows 1–4 for pattern.

DIRECTIONS

Back

With larger needles, CO 117 (127, 137, 147)(162, 172, 187, 197) sts. Beginning with a RS row, work Beaded Rib until piece measures 3″ from CO edge, ending with a WS row.

Dec Row (RS): K0 (0, 2, 0)(4, 4, 8, 4), *K8 (11, 15, 13)(10, 9, 8, 10), K2tog; rep from * to last 7 (10, 16, 12)(14, 14, 9, 13) sts, K to end. 11 (9, 7, 9)(12, 14, 17, 15) sts dec; 106 (118, 130, 138)(150, 158, 170, 182) sts.
Setup Row (WS): P1, PM, (P2, K2) to last st, PM, P1.
Next Row (RS): K1 (selvage st), SM, work Row 1 of Barter pattern to last st, SM, K1 (selvage st).
Maintaining first and last sts in St st, cont to work Barter pattern until piece measures 22.5 (23, 23.5, 24)(24.75, 25.75, 26.5, 27.25)″ from CO edge, ending with a RS row.

Next Row (WS): WE as established across 32 (38, 43, 46)(51, 55, 60, 65) sts, PM, WE as established across center 42 (42, 44, 46)(48, 48, 50, 52) sts, PM, work to end.

Shape Shoulders

Cont in pattern and BO 4 sts at beginning of next six rows. 82 (94, 106, 114)(126, 134, 146, 158) sts.

Neck

Next Row (RS): BO 4 sts, K to M, place sts between Ms on st holder or scrap yarn for neck. Place remaining 20 (26, 31, 34)(39, 43, 48, 53) sts on st holder or scrap yarn for left shoulder.

Right Shoulder

Next Row (WS): WE as established across WS row of remaining 16 (22, 27, 30)(35, 39, 44, 49) sts.
Cont in pattern while shaping: BO 4 sts at beginning of next two RS rows, then BO 2 (4, 4, 4)(8, 8, 8, 9) sts at beginning of next three RS rows, and then BO remaining 2 (2, 7, 10)(3, 7, 12, 14) sts.

Left Shoulder

Return shoulder sts to needles, join yarn to work a RS row.
Next Row (RS): K across.
Cont in pattern while shaping: BO 4 sts at beginning of next three WS rows, then BO 2 (4, 4, 4)(8, 8, 8, 9) sts at beginning of next three WS rows, and then BO remaining 2 (2, 7, 10)(3, 7, 12, 14) sts.

Front

Work same as Back until piece measures 21 (21.5, 22, 22.5)(23.5, 24.25, 25, 25.75)″ from CO edge, ending with a WS row.

Neck

Next Row (RS): WE as established across 42 (48, 54, 58)(63, 67, 72, 78) sts, place center 22 (22, 22, 22)(24, 24, 26, 26) sts on st holder or scrap yarn for neck, place remaining sts on st holder or scrap yarn for right shoulder.

Left Shoulder & Neck

Next Row (WS): From neck edge, BO 0 (0, 1, 2)(2, 2, 2, 3) sts, WE as established to end. 42 (48, 53, 56)(61, 65, 70, 75) sts.
Dec Row (RS): K to last 3 sts, K2tog, K1. 1 st dec.
Next Row (WS): P2, WE as established to end.
Rep last two rows three more times. 38 (44, 49, 52)(57, 61, 66, 71) sts.

Next Row (RS): BO 4 sts, K to last 3 sts, K2tog, K1. 33 (39, 44, 47)(52, 56, 61, 66) sts.
Next Row (WS): P2, WE as established to end.
Rep last two rows five more times. 8 (14, 19, 22)(27, 31, 36, 41) sts. This ends neck shaping.
Cont in pattern while shaping shoulder: BO 2 (4, 4, 4)(8, 8, 8, 9) sts at beginning of next three RS rows, and then BO remaining 2 (2, 7, 10)(3, 7, 12, 14) sts.

Right Shoulder & Neck

Return 42 (48, 54, 58)(63, 67, 72, 78) sts on hold for right shoulder to needles, rejoin yarn and with RS facing, BO 0 (0, 1, 2)(2, 2, 2, 3) sts, WE as established to end. 42 (48, 53, 56)(61, 65, 70, 75) sts.
WE as established across WS row.

Dec Row (RS): K1, SSK, K to end. 1 st dec.
Next Row (WS): WE as established to last 2 sts, P2.
Rep last two rows two more times, and then rep Dec Row once more. 38 (44, 49, 52)(57, 61, 66, 71) sts.

Next Row (WS): BO 4 sts, WE as established to last 2 sts, P2. 34 (39, 45, 48)(53, 57, 62, 67) sts.
Next Row (RS): K1, SSK, K to end. 1 st dec.
Rep last two rows five more times. 8 (14, 19, 22)(27, 31, 36, 41) sts. This ends neck shaping.
Cont in pattern while shaping shoulder: BO 2 (4, 4, 4)(8, 8, 8, 9) sts at beginning of next three WS rows, and then BO remaining 2 (2, 7, 10)(3, 7, 12, 14) sts.

Sleeves (make two the same)

With larger needles, CO 57 (57, 57, 57)(62, 62, 62, 62) sts.
Beginning with a RS row, work Beaded Rib until piece measures 3″ from CO edge, ending with a WS row.
Dec Row (RS): K9 (9, 9, 9)(1, 1, 1, 1), K2tog 1 (1, 1, 1)(0, 0, 0, 0) time(s), *K17 (17, 17, 17)(13, 13, 13, 13), K2tog; rep from * to last 8 (8, 8, 8)(1, 1, 1, 1) sts, K to end. 54 (54, 54, 54)(58, 58, 58, 58) sts.
Setup Row (WS): P1, PM, (P2, K2) to last st, PM, P1.
Next Row (RS): K1 (selvage st), SM, work Row 1 of Barter pattern to last st, SM, K1 (selvage st).
Maintaining first and last st in St st, cont in Barter pattern until piece measures 3.5″ from CO edge, end with a WS row.

Inc Row (RS): K1, M1R, K to last st, M1L, K1. 2 sts inc.
Rep Inc Row every 36 (26, 18, 14)(12, 8, 6, 4) rows 3 (4, 5, 5)(3, 5, 10, 21) times, then every 0 (0, 16, 12)(10, 6, 4, 2) rows 0 (0, 1, 3)(7, 11, 10, 3) time(s). 62 (64, 68, 72)(80, 92, 100, 108) sts.
WE in established pattern until sleeve measures 18.5 (18.25, 18.25, 18)(18, 18, 17.25, 16)″, ending with a WS row.
BO all sts.

Finishing

Block pieces to measurements in schematics.
Sew shoulder seams. Place removable M or safety pin 6 (6, 6.5, 6.75)(7.5, 8.75, 9.5, 10.25)″ down length of body from shoulder seam on both front and back pieces. Set in sleeves between markers and seam. Sew sleeve and side seams.

Neck

With smaller circular needle, beginning at left shoulder seam, PU and K 16 sts along neck, K22 (22, 22, 22)(24, 24, 26, 26) held front sts, PU and K 16 sts to shoulder seam, PU and K 7 sts along neck, K42 (42, 44, 46)(48, 48, 50, 52) held back sts, PU and K 7 sts to end. PM and join in the rnd. 110 (110, 112, 114)(118, 118, 122, 124) sts.
Work 1x1 Rib for five rnds.
Knit seven rnds.
Loosely BO all sts. Allow neck edge to curl.

LEGEND

K
RS: Knit stitch
WS: Purl stitch

P
RS: Purl stitch
WS: Knit stitch

Pattern Repeat

Barter

Beaded Rib

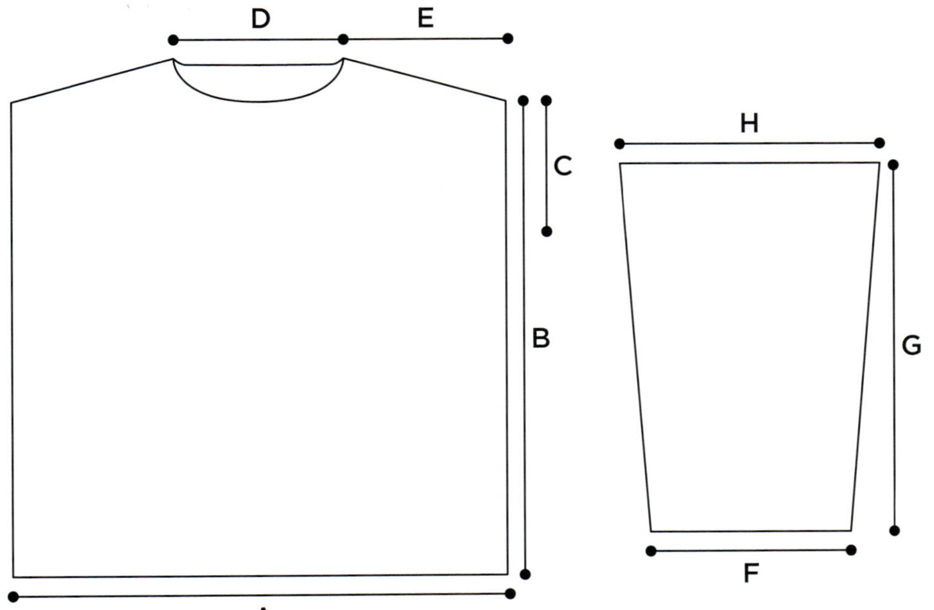

A 20.25 (22.5, 24.75, 26.25)(28.5, 30, 32.5, 34.75)″

B 22.5 (23, 23.5, 24)(24.75, 25.75, 26.5, 27.25)″

C 6 (6, 6.5, 6.75)(7.5, 8.75, 9.5, 10.25)″

D 8 (8, 8.5, 8.75)(9.25, 9.25, 9.5, 10)″

E 6 (7.25, 8.25, 8.75)(9.75, 10.5, 11.5, 12.5)″

F 10 (10, 10, 10)(10.75, 10.75, 10.75, 10.75)″

G 18.5 (18.25, 18.25, 18)(18, 18, 17.25, 16)″

H 11.75 (12.25, 13, 13.75)(15.25, 17.5, 19, 20.5)″

ANGUILA SWEATER

by Kirsten Joel

FINISHED MEASUREMENTS

34 (37, 40, 43, 46, 49.25)(53, 56.75, 59.75, 62.75, 66.75)" finished bust circumference; meant to be worn with 2–4" positive ease
Sample is 37" size; model is 33.5" bust

YARN

Twill™ (worsted weight, 100% Superwash Merino Wool; 149 yards/ 100g): Overcast 27936, 7 (8, 9, 10, 10, 11)(12, 13, 14, 14, 15) hanks

NEEDLES

US 6 (4mm) straight or circular needles (24" or longer), or size to obtain gauge
US 5 (3.75mm) 24" circular needles, or one size smaller than size used to obtain gauge

NOTIONS

Yarn Needle
Stitch Markers
Stitch Holder or Scrap Yarn
Blocking Pins and/or Wires

GAUGE

21 sts and 30 rows = 4" in Stockinette Stitch on larger needles, blocked

For pattern support, contact kirstenfjoel@kleverknitsdesigns.com

Anguila Sweater

Notes:
Anguila is a fun take on the traditional crew neck sweater. The classic shape is accented with a sleek slip stitch pattern that deserves to be center stage in your fall wardrobe.

Set-in sleeves provide an easy and flattering fit. The front and back are knit from the bottom up, back and forth in rows. Once the pieces are all knit, they are blocked and seamed together before knitting the neckband.

Slip Stitch Pattern (flat over a multiple of 4 sts plus 3)
Row 1 (RS): K1, (Sl1 WYIB, P3) to last 2 sts, Sl1 WYIB, K1.
Row 2 (WS): K1, (P1, K3) to last 2 sts, P1, K1.
Rep Rows 1–2 for pattern.

DIRECTIONS

Back
With larger needles, CO 91 (99, 107, 115, 123, 131)(141, 151, 159, 167, 177) sts.
Work Slip Stitch Pattern for four rows.
On subsequent rows, work partial rep of Slip Stitch pattern as needed.
Row 1 (RS): K1, (Sl1 WYIB, P3) to last 3 sts, K2tog, M1, K1.
Row 2 (WS): K1, P1, (P1, K3) to last 2 sts, P1, K1.
Row 3: K1, (Sl1 WYIB, P3) to last 4 sts, K2tog, M1, K2.
Row 4: K1, P2, (P1, K3) to last 2 sts, P1, K1.
Row 5: K1, (Sl1 WYIB, P3) to last 5 sts, K2tog, M1, K2.
Row 6: K1, P3, (P1, K3) to last 2 sts, P1, K1.
Cont as established, working Slip Stitch pattern one fewer st on each subsequent RS row, until piece measures 16.25 (16.25, 16.75, 16.75, 17.25, 17.25)(17.25, 17, 16.75, 16.5, 16.5)" from CO edge, ending after a WS row.

Shape Armhole
BO 3 (4, 5, 6, 8, 9)(11, 12, 13, 14, 14) sts at beginning of next two rows. 85 (91, 97, 103, 107, 113)(119, 127, 133, 139, 149) sts.
Armhole Dec Row (RS): K1, SSK, work as established to last 3 sts, K2tog, K1. 2 sts dec.
Cont as established and rep Armhole Dec Row every RS row 5 (5, 6, 6, 6, 7)(8, 9, 11, 12, 15) more times. 73 (79, 83, 89, 93, 97)(101, 107, 109, 113, 117) sts.

WE until armhole measures 6.25 (6.75, 7.25, 7.75, 8.25, 8.75)(8.75, 9, 9.25, 9.5, 9.75)" from armhole BO.

Shape Neck
Work 16 (18, 19, 22, 23, 24)(25, 28, 28, 30, 31) sts, join second ball of yarn and BO center 41 (43, 45, 45, 47, 49)(51, 51, 53, 53, 55) sts, work to end. 16 (18, 19, 22, 23, 24)(25, 28, 28, 30, 31) sts for each shoulder.

You will now work across both shoulders at the same time.
Next Row (WS): WE across all sts.
Dec Row (RS): Work to last 3 sts of RH shoulder, K2tog, K1; K1, SSK, work to end. 1 st dec each side.
Next Row: WE across all sts.

Rep last two rows once more. 14 (16, 17, 20, 21, 22)(23, 26, 26, 28, 29) sts.
BO all sts.

Front
Work as for Back through Shape Armhole. WE until armhole measures 3.25 (3.25, 3.75, 3.75, 4.25, 4.5)(4.5, 4.5, 4.75, 5, 5)" from armhole BO. 73 (79, 83, 89, 93, 97)(101, 107, 109, 113, 117) sts.

Shape Neck
Work 18 (20, 21, 24, 25, 26)(27, 30, 30, 32, 33) sts, join second ball of yarn and BO center 37 (39, 41, 41, 43, 45)(47, 47, 49, 49, 51) sts, work as established to end. 18 (20, 21, 24, 25, 26)(27, 30, 30, 32, 33) sts for each side.
Next Row (WS): WE across all sts.
Dec Row (RS): Work to last 3 sts of LH shoulder, K2tog, K1; K1, SSK, work to end. 1 st dec each side.
Cont as established and rep Dec Row every RS row three more times. 14 (16, 17, 20, 21, 22)(23, 26, 26, 28, 29) sts.
WE as established until armhole measures 7 (7.5, 8, 8.5, 9, 9.5)(9.5, 9.75, 10, 10.25, 10.5)" from armhole BO, ending after a WS row.
BO all sts.

Sleeves (make two the same)
With larger needles, CO 43 (47, 47, 47, 51, 51)(51, 51, 55, 55, 55) sts.
Work Slip Stitch Pattern for 3".
Inc Row (RS): K2, M1, K to last 2 sts, M1, K2. 2 sts inc.
Work St st and rep Inc Row every 16 (16, 12, 10, 10, 8)(8, 6, 6, 6, 6) rows 4 (6, 3, 7, 3, 7)(1, 10, 10, 7, 4) more times, then every 14 (0, 10, 8, 8, 6)(6, 4, 4, 4, 4) rows 2 (0, 6, 4, 9, 8)(16, 10, 10, 14, 18) times. 57 (61, 67, 71, 77, 83)(87, 93, 97, 99, 101) sts.

WE until piece measures 18 (18.5, 18.5, 18.75, 18.75, 19)(19, 19, 18.75, 18.75, 18.5)" from CO edge, ending with a WS row.

Shape Sleeve Cap
BO 3 (4, 5, 6, 8, 9)(11, 12, 13, 14, 14) sts at beginning of next two rows. 51 (53, 57, 59, 61, 65)(65, 69, 71, 71, 73) sts.
Dec Row (RS): K1, SSK, work to last 3 sts, K2tog, K1. 2 sts dec.
Work Dec Row every other row 4 (5, 5, 6, 5, 6)(6, 6, 7, 6, 7) more times, then every four rows 2 (2, 2, 2, 3, 3)(3, 1, 1, 2, 2) times, then every other row 3 (3, 4, 4, 4, 4)(4, 7, 7, 6, 6) times. 31 (31, 33, 33, 35, 37)(37, 39, 39, 41, 41) sts.
WE one row (WS).
Double Dec Row (RS): K1, SK2P, K to last 4 sts, K3tog, K1. 4 sts dec.
Rep Double Dec Row every other row three more times. 15 (15, 17, 17, 19, 21)(21, 23, 23, 25, 25) sts.
WE one row (WS).
BO all sts.

Finishing
Weave in ends, wash, and block to diagram.
Sew sides seams, shoulder seams, and sleeves; set in sleeves to armhole.

Neckband

With smaller circular needle, RS facing, and beginning at RH shoulder, PU and K: 3 sts along back neck, 41 (43, 45, 45, 47, 49)(51, 51, 53, 53, 55) sts evenly along back neck BO row, 3 sts along back neck, 18 (20, 20, 21, 21, 22)(22, 22, 24, 26, 26) sts even along left side of front neck, 37 (39, 41, 41, 43, 45)(47, 47, 49, 49, 51) sts along front neck BO, 18 (20, 20, 21, 21, 22)(22, 22, 24, 26, 26) sts along RH side of front neck. 120 (128, 132, 134, 138, 144)(148, 148, 156, 160, 164) sts.

Join for working in the rnd and work 1x1 Rib until neckband measures 1″ from PU row.
BO in pattern.

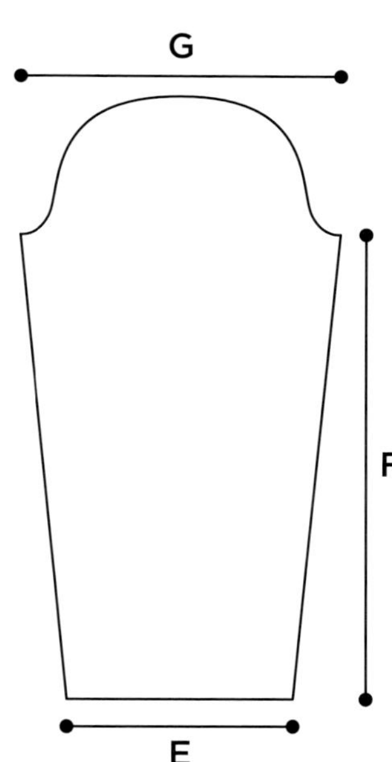

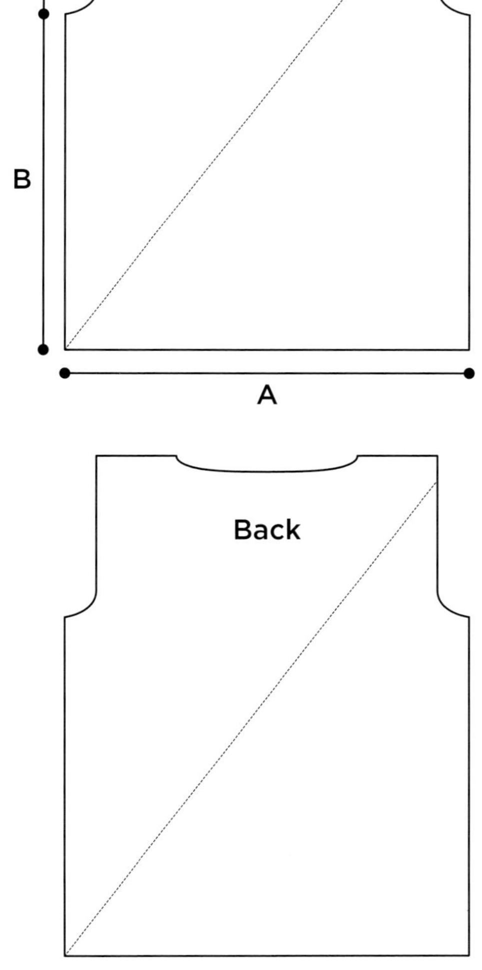

A   17.25 (18.75, 20.25, 22, 23.5, 25)(26.75, 28.75, 30.25, 31.75, 33.75)″
B   16.25 (16.25, 16.75, 16.75, 17.25, 17.25)(17.25, 17, 16.75, 16.5, 16.5)″
C   7 (7.5, 8, 8.5, 9, 9.5)(9.5, 9.75, 10, 10.25, 10.5)″
D   2.75 (3, 3.25, 3.75, 4.25, 4.5)(4.5, 5, 5, 5.25, 5.5)″
E   8.25 (9, 9, 9, 9.75, 9.75)(9.75, 9.75, 10.5, 10.5, 10.5)″
F   18 (18.5, 18.5, 18.75, 18.75, 19) (19, 19, 18.75, 18.75, 18.5)″
G   10.75 (11.5, 12.75, 13.5, 14.75, 15.75)(16.5, 17.75, 18.5, 18.75, 19.25)″

AUTUMN HARVEST SLOUCH HAT

by Emily Kintigh

FINISHED MEASUREMENTS

18.75 (20.75, 23)" circumference; meant to be worn with approx 2–3" negative ease (*sample is 20.75" size*)

YARN

Stroll™ Tweed (fingering weight, 65% Fine Superwash Merino Wool, 25% Nylon, 10% Donegal Tweed; 231 yards/50g): Barley Heather 28194, 1 (2, 2) skeins

NEEDLES

US 3 (3.25mm) DPNs or two 24" circular needles for two circulars technique or 32" or longer circular needles for Magic Loop technique, or size to obtain gauge

US 2 (2.75mm) DPNs or two 24" circular needles for two circulars technique or 32" or longer circular needles for Magic Loop technique, or one size smaller than size used to obtain gauge

NOTIONS

Yarn Needle
Stitch Markers

GAUGE

23 sts and 70 rnds = 4" over Harvest Chart in the round on larger needles, blocked

For pattern support, contact auntieemsstudio@gmail.com

Autumn Harvest Slouch Hat

Notes:

The beautifully textured hat features a broken up Fisherman's Rib pattern resembling rows of crops. It makes a lovely, loose, and squishy fabric that is ideal for a slouchy hat.

The Autumn Harvest Slouch Hat is worked in the round from the brim up. The brim is worked in 1x1 Rib; stitches are then decreased before beginning the main pattern because the stitch pattern makes such a loose, stretchy fabric. The pattern is made by knitting and purling into the stitch below.

When blocking, the fabric can stretch quite a bit. For best results, lay the hat flat, then shape gently as needed.

For an extra slouchy hat, work the size matching the head circumference it is to fit.

When checking round gauge, counting chart repeats is easier than trying to count the stitches of the pattern.

Charts are worked in the round; read each chart row from right to left as a RS row.

DIRECTIONS

Brim

With smaller needles, loosely CO 144 (160, 176) sts. PM and join to work in the rnd, being careful not to twist sts. Work 1x1 Rib until piece measures 1″ from CO edge.

Body

Switch to larger needles.
Setup Rnd: (K1, P1, P2tog) to end. 108 (120, 132) sts.
Next Rnd: P all.
Begin working from Harvest chart. Work Rnds 1–10 of Harvest chart 7 (8, 9) times, then work another 8 (4, 0) rnds of chart.

Crown

Crown chart is repeated six times across the rnd. If desired, PMs every 18 (20, 22) sts on first rnd worked to keep track of chart reps.
Begin working from Crown chart, starting on Rnd 9 (5, 1) of chart and working through Rnd 41. 6 sts.
Break yarn and pull through remaining sts.

Finishing

Weave in ends, wash, and block.

LEGEND

- No Stitch — Placeholder—no stitch made
- Knit Stitch
- Purl Stitch
- Knit in stitch below
- Purl in stitch below
- K2tog — Knit 2 stitches together as one stitch
- Start for 23″ size
- Start for 20.75″ size
- Start for 18.75″ size

Harvest

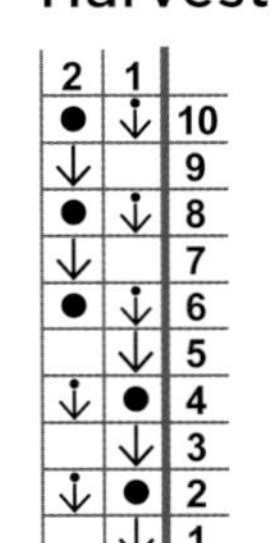

Crown

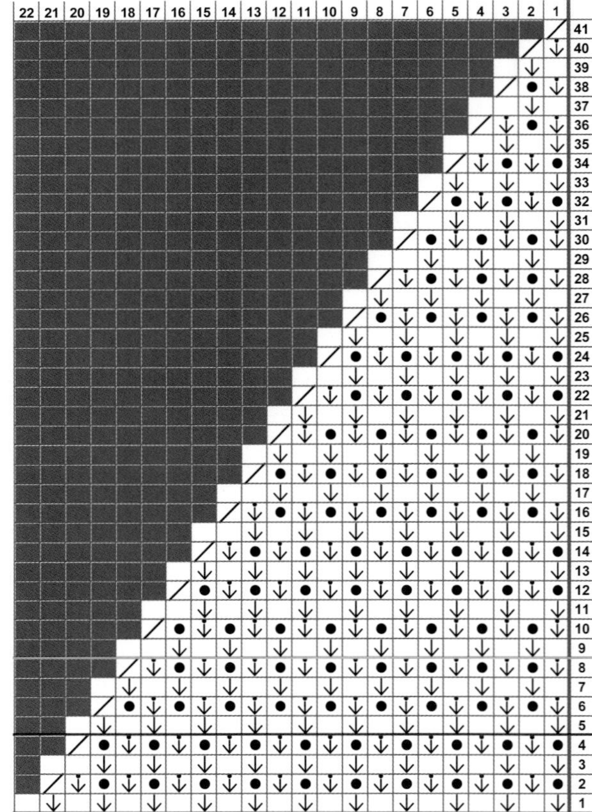

ECHOES MITTENS

by Moira Engel

FINISHED MEASUREMENTS

6.5 (7.75, 9)" hand circumference,
5.75 (7, 8.25)" cuff circumference ×
9 (10, 10.5)" height (*sample is 7.75" size*)

YARN

Twill™ (worsted weight, 100% Superwash
Merino Wool; 149 yards/100g):
MC Black Cherry Heather 27928, 1 (2,
2) hanks; CC Horchata 27936, 1 hank

NEEDLES

US 2.5 (3mm) DPNs, or size to obtain
gauge

NOTIONS

Yarn Needle
Stitch Markers
Stitch Holders or Scrap Yarn
Blocking Pins
Cable Needle (optional)

GAUGE

22 sts and 36 rnds = 4" in Stockinette
Stitch in the round, blocked
24 sts and 36 rnds = 4" in Right Twist
pattern in the round, blocked
24 sts and 36 rnds = 4" in Half Linen
pattern in the round, blocked

Echoes Mittens

Notes:

The inspiration for these mittens is texture and sound. With an initial clap of color, the echoes are twisted stitches. Intense repeating texture creates a three dimensional cozy pair of mittens.

Echoes Mittens are worked in the round from the cuff up. The color section is an attractive yet simple Half Linen slipped stitch pattern. The palm is worked in Stockinette Stitch, and the twisted stitch can be worked without a cable needle.

Half Linen is a slipped stitch pattern. Rounds 1 and 2 are worked only with the contrasting color, while Rounds 3 and 4 are worked with the main color. The slipped stitches make the texture and color pattern. Be sure to slip stitches with yarn held in front to create the woven look.

Charts are worked in the round; read each chart row from right to left as a RS row.

RT (right twist)
Work without a cable needle: K into second st on LH needle, K TBL into first st, then slip both sts off needle tog.
Or work with a cable needle: Sl first st to CN and hold to back, K1, then K1 TBL from CN.

DIRECTIONS

Right Mitten
Cuff
Using MC, loosely CO 36 (44, 52) sts. PM and join to work in the rnd, being careful not to twist sts.
Work 2x2 Rib for 1 (1, 1.5)".
At end of final rnd of ribbing, inc 1 st using M1. 37 (45, 53) sts.
Next Rnd: Using MC, K all.

Half Linen Section
Join CC and work Half Linen chart Rnds 1–4 five times. Break CC.
Next Rnd: Using MC, M1 (0, 0), K19 (23, 26), PM for side, M1 (0, 0), K18 (22, 27). 39 (45, 53) sts.

Body
Setup Rnd: K2, work Right Twist chart 5 (6, 7) times, P1, K2, SM, K19 (22, 27) palm sts to end.
WE in pattern as established until piece measures 2.5 (2.5, 3)" from CO edge.

Gusset
Setup Rnd: Work in pattern to side M, SM, K1 (1, 2), PM for gusset, K2, PM for gusset, K to end.
Rnd 1: Work in pattern to gusset M, SM, M1R, K to next gusset M, M1L, SM, K to end. 2 gusset sts inc.
Rnd 2: WE in pattern.
Rep Rnds 1–2 until there are 16 (18, 20) sts between gusset Ms. 53 (61, 71) sts.
WE in pattern until piece measures 6 (6.5, 7)" from CO edge.

Next Rnd: Work to first gusset M, remove M, M1L, move 16 (18, 20) thumb sts onto st holder or scrap yarn, M1R, remove second gusset M, work to end. 39 (45, 53) sts.
WE in pattern until mitten measures 7.75 (8.5, 8.75)" from CO edge. On final rnd, work to 2 sts before M, K2tog, SM, work to end. 38 (44, 52) sts.

Top of Mitten
Rnd 1: K2, SSK, work in pattern to 4 sts before side M, K2tog, K2, SM, K2, SSK, K to 4 sts before end M, K2tog, K2. 4 sts dec.
Rnd 2: WE in pattern.
Rep Rnds 1–2 until 14 (16, 20) sts remain.
Graft live sts tog using Kitchener Stitch.

Thumb
Move 16 (18, 20) gusset sts from holder onto DPNs. PU and K 2 sts from body of mittens, PM and join to work in the rnd. 18 (20, 22) sts.
Work St st until thumb measures 1.75 (2, 2.25)" from crook of thumb.

Top of Thumb
Rnd 1: (K2tog) to end. 9 (10, 11) sts.
Rnd 2: K all.
Rnd 3: (K2tog) to last 1 (0, 1) st, K1 (0, 1). 5 (5, 6) sts.
Break yarn, leaving a long enough tail to close thumb. Using a yarn needle, bring yarn through remaining sts and pull to close top of thumb. Fasten off.

Left Mitten
Work as for Right Mitten, until Gusset.

Gusset
Setup Rnd: Work in pattern to 3 (3, 4) sts before end M, PM for gusset, K2, PM for gusset, K1 (1, 2) to end.

Work remainder of Mitten as for Right Mitten.

Finishing
Weave in ends, wash, and block as desired.

LEGEND

Half Linen

Right Twist

☐	Main Color	☐ Knit Stitch
▨	Contrasting Color	⊡ Purl Stitch
☑	Sl WYIF — Slip stitch purl-wise, with yarn in front	
⧖	Right Twist (RT) — Sl1 to CN, hold in back; K1, K1 from CN	
▱	Pattern Repeat	

FISHERMAN'S WEAVE HAT

by Holli Yeoh

FINISHED MEASUREMENTS

17.5 (20, 22.5)" circumference × 7.5 (8.25, 8.5)" height for beanie version or 9.25 (10.25, 11)" height for slouchy version; meant to be worn with approx 10%–15% negative ease—choose a finished size 2–3" smaller than head (*sample is 20" size*)

YARN

Swish™ (DK weight, 100% Fine Superwash Merino Wool; 123 yards/50g): Delft Heather 24312, 2 (2, 3) skeins

NEEDLES

US 5 (3.75mm) DPNs and 16" circular needles or two 24" circular needles for two circulars technique or 32" or longer circular needles for Magic Loop technique, or size to obtain gauge

US 4 (3.5mm) 16" circular needles or two 24" circular needles for two circulars technique or 32" or longer circular needles for Magic Loop technique, or one size smaller than size used to obtain gauge

NOTIONS

Yarn Needle
Stitch Markers
8 or 12cm Faux Fur Pom-Pom (optional)

GAUGE

16 sts and 46 rnds = 4" in Fisherman's Rib in the round on larger needles, blocked and relaxed
18 sts and 48 rnds = 4" in Fisherman's Rib in the round on larger needles, unblocked and relaxed

For pattern support, contact info@holliyeoh.com

Fisherman's Weave Hat

Notes:

Two simple textures combine in a cozy, insulating hat. Working Garter Stitch ridges into a Fisherman's Rib body creates strong visual interest with no fuss. Clean lines, warm, washable yarn, and a good range of sizes make this a unisex winner; keep it ruggedly plain or add a fluffy pom-pom to soften the look.

Fisherman's Rib is the often-overlooked cousin to Brioche—it's simpler to work but creates the same dense, squishy structure. The hat is worked in the round from the bottom up.

Yardage estimates are for the slouchy version and include enough yarn for a pom-pom.

When working Fisherman's Rib, there are two rows worked for every visible knit stitch. To determine round gauge, count the stitches in a column of knit stitches and multiply by two.

This fabric and yarn combination relaxes when blocked. Block gauge swatch for best results. Length measurements in the directions are unblocked.

Tip: If you lose your place, to determine pattern round, look at the next stitch in the round below the sts on the left-hand needle. If two strands make up the purl bump, work into the next stitch on the needle (K1 or P1). If only one strand makes up the purl bump, work into that stitch (K1B or P1B).

K1B (knit 1 below)
Knit into st directly below next st on needle, allowing next st to drop off needle: from front to back, insert RH needle through center of st in the row directly below next st on needle, wrap yarn around needle and complete.

P1B (purl 1 below)
Purl into st directly below next st on needle, allowing next st to drop off needle.

Fisherman's Rib (in the round over an even number of sts)
Rnd 1: (K1B, P1) to end of rnd.
Rnd 2: (K1, P1B) to end of rnd.
Rep Rnds 1–2 for pattern.

Woven Pattern (in the round over a multiple of 10 sts)
Rnd 1: (K1B, P1, K1B, K7) to end of rnd.
Rnd 2: (K1, P1B, K1, P7) to end of rnd.
Rep Rnds 1–2 for pattern.

DIRECTIONS

Ribbed Brim
With smaller needles, CO 70 (80, 90) sts.
PM for BOR and join to work in the rnd, taking care not to twist sts.
Rnd 1: Placing Ms every 10 sts, (K1, P1) to end of rnd. 6 (7, 8) Ms between reps plus one for BOR.
Work Fisherman's Rib for 14 rnds.

Woven Texture
Change to larger needles.
Work Woven Pattern for 12 (12, 14) rnds.

Fisherman's Rib Upper Body
Next Rnd: *(K1B, P1) two times, (K1, P1) three times; rep from * 6 (7, 8) more times.
Beginning and ending with Rnd 2, work Fisherman's Rib until hat measures approx 5.5 (6.25, 6.5)" from CO edge for Beanie version or 7 (8, 8.75)" from CO for Slouchy version.

Crown
If using 16" circular needle, change to DPNs when there are too few sts to fit comfortably on circular cord.
Rnd 1: *(K1B, P1) to 4 sts before M, K3tog, P1; rep from * to end of rnd. 14 (16, 18) sts dec.
Rnds 2–6: Work Fisherman's Rib, beginning with Rnd 2 of pattern.
Rnds 7–18: Rep Rnds 1–6 two more times. 28 (32, 36) sts; 4 sts between Ms.
Rnd 19: (K3tog, P1, remove M) to end (do not remove BOR M). 14 (16, 18) sts.
Rnd 20: (K1, P1B) to end of rnd, remove BOR M, K1B, PM. M indicates new BOR.
Rnd 21: (K2tog) to end of rnd. 7 (8, 9) sts.
Break yarn, leaving an 8" tail, and thread through remaining sts. Pull tightly and secure end.

Finishing
Weave in ends, wash, and block to dimensions.

Pom-Pom (optional)
Make a 4" pom-pom or use a faux fur pom-pom and secure to top of hat.

MISTY COWL

by Stana D. Sortor

FINISHED MEASUREMENTS

25.25″ circumference × 15″ height

YARN

Stroll™ Tonal (fingering weight, 75% Fine Superwash Merino Wool, 25% Nylon; 462 yards/100g): MC Inverness 26750, 1 hank

and

Stroll™ Tonal Mini Pack (fingering weight, 75% Fine Superwash Merino Wool, 25% Nylon; 462 yards/100g total): Spring Fields Mini Pack 44542 (C1 Evergreen, C2 Mountain Pass, C3 Cold Stream, C4 Eucalyptus, C5 Pearlescent), 1 pack

NEEDLES

US 7 (4.5mm) 24″ circular needles, or size to obtain gauge

NOTIONS

Yarn Needle
Stitch Marker

GAUGE

19 sts and 34 rnds = 4″ in Loop Pattern in the round with yarns held together, blocked

For pattern support, contact crowsd@yahoo.com

Misty Cowl

Notes:

This super soft cowl is work in the round.

Start with a Long Tail Cast On, then work the Loop Pattern with yarns held together, playing with Stroll Tonal mini skeins for a marbled effect.

Loop Pattern (in the round over a multiple of 2 sts)
Rnd 1: K all.
Rnd 2: P1, Sl1 WYIF.
Rnd 3: K all.
Rnd 4: Sl1 WYIF, P1.
Rep Rnds 1–4 for pattern.

DIRECTIONS

With MC and C1 yarns held tog, using Long Tail Cast On, loosely CO 120 sts. PM for BOR and join to work in the rnd, being careful not to twist sts.

Work Loop Pattern with yarns held tog, changing the CC yarn as follows.
Rnds 1–16: Work in MC and C1. Join C2.
Rnds 17–18: Work in MC and C2.
Rnds 19–20: Work in MC and C1.
Rnds 21–22: Work in MC and C2.
Rnds 23–24: Work in MC and C1.
Rnds 25–26: Work in MC and C2.
Rnds 27–28: Work in MC and C1. Break C1.

Rnds 29–44: Work in MC and C2. Join C3.
Rnds 45–46: Work in MC and C3.
Rnds 47–48: Work in MC and C2.
Rnds 49–50: Work in MC and C3.
Rnds 51–52: Work in MC and C2.
Rnds 53–54: Work in MC and C3.
Rnds 55–56: Work in MC and C2. Break C2.
Rnds 57–72: Work in MC and C3. Join C4.
Rnds 73–74: Work in MC and C4.
Rnds 75–76: Work in MC and C3.
Rnds 77–78: Work in MC and C4.
Rnds 79–80: Work in MC and C3.
Rnds 81–82: Work in MC and C4.
Rnds 83–84: Work in MC and C3. Break C3.
Rnds 85–100: Work in MC and C4. Join C5.
Rnds 101–102: Work in MC and C5.
Rnds 103–104: Work in MC and C4.
Rnds 105–106: Work in MC and C5.
Rnds 107–108: Work in MC and C4.
Rnds 109–110: Work in MC and C5.
Rnds 111–112: Work in MC and C4. Break C4.
Rnds 113–128: Work in MC and C5.
BO loosely with MC and C5.

Finishing

Weave in ends, wash, and block to measurements.

MOSS STITCH CHECK JUMPER

by Helen Metcalfe

FINISHED MEASUREMENTS

33 (37.75, 41.5, 45.25, 49)(53.75, 57.5, 61.25, 65)" finished bust circumference; meant to be worn with 4–6" positive ease
Sample is 41.5" size; model is 33.5" bust

YARN

Swish™ (worsted weight, 100% Fine Superwash Merino Wool; 110 yards/50g): Copper 23882, 10 (10, 11, 13, 14)(15, 16, 17, 18) skeins

NEEDLES

US 7 (4.5mm) straight or circular needles (24" or longer) and DPNs or two 24" circular needles for two circulars technique, or size to obtain gauge

US 8 (5mm) straight or circular needles (24" or longer), or size to obtain gauge

NOTIONS

Yarn Needle
Stitch Marker
2 Stitch Holders or Scrap Yarn
Blocking Pins and/or Wires

GAUGE

17 sts and 29 rows = 4" in Moss Stitch Check on larger needles, blocked
17 sts and 24 rows = 4" in 1x1 Rib on smaller needles, blocked (note that this is approximate due to the amount of stretch in the ribbing)

Moss Stitch Check Jumper

Notes:

A rhythmic stitch pattern was the perfect starting point for this design. Combined with Swish Worsted, the result is a cozy wardrobe staple.

The Moss Stitch Check Jumper has a drop sleeve shoulder construction, resulting in minimal shaping to interrupt the stitch pattern, which is worked all over. The pullover is worked in four pieces, flat from the bottom up; after the shoulders are joined, stitches for the neckband are picked up and worked in the round.

Charts are worked flat; read RS rows (odd numbers) from right to left, and WS rows (even numbers) from left to right.

Moss Stitch Check (flat over a multiple of 14 sts plus 2)
Row 1 (RS): K across.
Row 2 (WS): P2, *(K1, P1) two times, K1, P2; rep from * to end.
Row 3: *K3, P1, K1, P1, K4, (P1, K1) two times; rep from * to last 2 sts, K2.
Rows 4–7: Rep Rows 2–3 twice more.
Row 8: P2, (K12, P2) to end.
Row 9: (K2, P12) to last 2 sts, K2.
Row 10: P across.
Row 11: *K2, (P1, K1) two times, P1; rep from * to last 2 sts, K2.
Row 12: P2, *(P1, K1) two times, P4, K1, P1, K1, P3; rep from * to end.
Rows 13–16: Rep Rows 11–12 twice more.
Row 17: (P7, K2, P5) to last 2 sts, P2.
Row 18: K2, (K5, P2, K7) to end.
Rep Rows 1–18 for pattern.

DIRECTIONS

Back
**Using smaller needles, CO 72 (82, 90, 98, 106)(116, 124, 132, 140) sts.
Work 1x1 Rib for 2" from CO edge, ending after a WS row.

Switch to larger needles.
Row 1 (RS): P0 (5, 2, 6, 3)(1, 5, 2, 6), work Row 1 of Moss Stitch Check from chart or written instructions to last 0 (5, 2, 6, 3)(1, 5, 2, 6) sts, P to end.
Row 2 (WS): K0 (5, 2, 6, 3)(1, 5, 2, 6), work Row 2 of Moss Stitch Check to last 0 (5, 2, 6, 3)(1, 5, 2, 6) sts, K to end.**

Cont as established until Back measures 23.25 (23.5, 24.25, 25.5, 26.5)(28, 28.5, 29, 29.25)", ending after a WS row.
Cont as established and BO 4 (5, 6, 6, 7)(8, 9, 9, 10) sts at beginning of next 8 (6, 2, 8, 6)(4, 2, 8, 6) rows. 40 (52, 78, 50, 64)(84, 106, 60, 80) sts.
Cont as established and BO 3 (4, 5, 5, 6)(7, 8, 8, 9) sts at beginning of next 2 (4, 8, 2, 4)(6, 8, 2, 4) rows. 34 (36, 38, 40, 40)(42, 42, 44, 44) sts.
Place remaining sts on a st holder or scrap yarn.

Front
Work as for Back from ** to **.

Cont as established until Front measures 20.5 (20.75, 21.5, 22.75, 23.75)(25.25, 25.75, 26.25, 26.5)", ending after a WS row.
Next Row (RS): Work 32 (36, 39, 42, 46)(50, 54, 57, 61) sts, turn. Now work these sts only; place remaining 40 (46, 51, 56, 60)(66, 70, 75, 79) sts on st holder or scrap yarn.

Cont as established and BO 2 sts at beginning of next three WS rows. 26 (30, 33, 36, 40)(44, 48, 51, 55) sts.
Next Row (RS): Work as established to last 3 sts, K2tog, K1. 1 st dec.
Next Row (WS): WE as established.
Rep the last two rows six more times. 19 (23, 26, 29, 33)(37, 41, 44, 48) sts.
Cont as established and BO 4 (5, 6, 6, 7)(8, 9, 9, 10) sts at beginning of next 4 (3, 1, 4, 3)(2, 1, 4, 3) RS row(s), then BO 3 (4, 5, 5, 6)(7, 8, 8, 9) sts at beginning of next 1 (2, 4, 1, 2)(3, 4, 1, 2) RS row(s). All sts have been bound off.

With RS facing, leave center 8 (10, 12, 14, 14)(16, 16, 18, 18) sts on st holder and place 32 (36, 39, 42, 46)(50, 54, 57, 61) sts back onto larger needles.
Cont as established and BO 2 sts at beginning of next three RS rows. 26 (30, 33, 36, 40)(44, 48, 51, 55) sts.
Next Row (WS): WE as established.
Next Row (RS): K1, SSK, work in pattern to end. 1 st dec.
Rep the last two rows six more times. 19 (23, 26, 29, 33)(37, 41, 44, 48) sts.
Work two rows even.
Cont as established and BO 4 (5, 6, 6, 7)(8, 9, 9, 10) sts at beginning of next 4 (3, 1, 4, 3)(2, 1, 4, 3) WS row(s), then BO 3 (4, 5, 5, 6)(7, 8, 8, 9) sts at beginning of next 1 (2, 4, 1, 2)(3, 4, 1, 2) WS row(s). All sts have been bound off.

Sleeves (make two the same)
Using smaller needles, loosely CO 36 (38, 40, 44, 44)(46, 46, 48, 48) sts.
Work 1x1 Rib for 1.5" from CO edge, ending after a WS row.

Switch to larger needles.
Row 1 (RS): P3 (4, 5, 7, 7)(1, 1, 2, 2), work Row 1 of Moss Stitch Check to last 3 (4, 5, 7, 7)(1, 1, 2, 2) sts, P to end.
Row 2 (WS): K3 (4, 5, 7, 7)(1, 1, 2, 2), work Row 2 of Moss Stitch Check to last 3 (4, 5, 7, 7)(1, 1, 2, 2) sts, K to end.

As shaping progresses, incorporate new sts into Moss Stitch Check. Keep 1 st on each edge as a selvage st by working first and last st in rev St st: P on RS rows, K on WS rows.

Inc Row (RS): P1, M1, work as established to last st, M1, P1. 2 sts inc.
Cont as established, rep Inc Row every 16 (16, 16, 14, 10)(8, 6, 6, 6) rows 6 (6, 6, 7, 10)(13, 17, 18, 18) more times. 50 (52, 54, 60, 66)(74, 82, 86, 86) sts.
Cont without shaping until work measures 17.75" from CO edge, ending after a WS row.
BO remaining sts.

Neckband

Seam shoulders.

With RS facing and smaller needles, PU and K 20 sts down left front neckline, K8 (10, 12, 14, 14)(16, 16, 18, 18) sts from front st holder, PU and K 20 sts up right front neckline, K34 (36, 38, 40, 40)(42, 42, 44, 44) sts from back st holder. PM to mark BOR. 82 (86, 90, 94, 94)(98, 98, 102, 102) sts. Starting with a knit st, work 1x1 Rib until Neckband measures 1".
BO loosely in pattern.

Finishing

Line up center of top of sleeve cap with shoulder seam, sew tog using Mattress st.
Rep for other sleeve.
Sew sleeve and side seams.
Weave in ends, wash, and block to diagram.

Moss Stitch Check

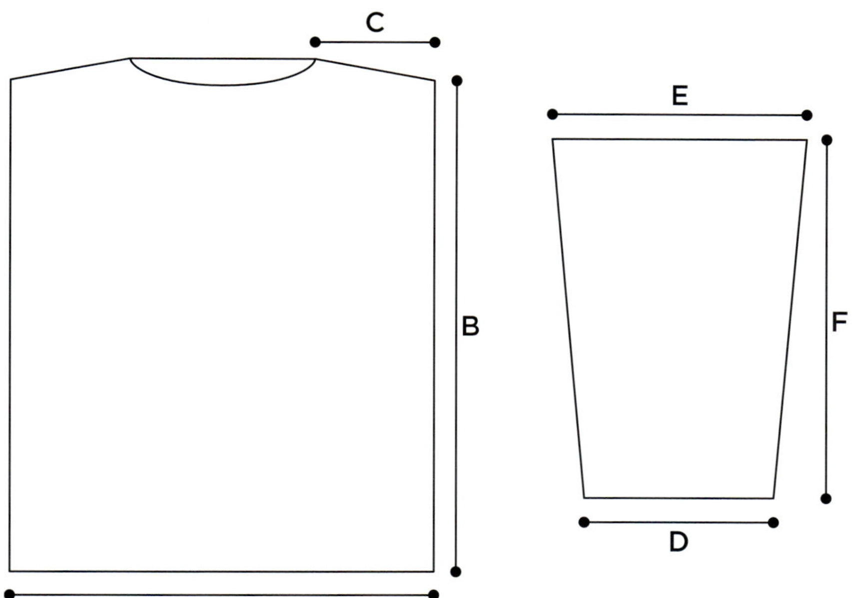

PALORA PULLOVER

by Kristen TenDyke

FINISHED MEASUREMENTS

37 (40.75, 44.25, 48, 51.75)(55.25, 59, 61.5, 65, 67.75)" finished bust circumference; meant to be worn with 3–5" positive ease
Sample is 40.75" size; model is 33.5" bust

YARN

Swish™ (DK weight, 100% Fine Superwash Merino Wool; 123 yards/50g) Amethyst Heather 24310, 12 (13, 14, 16, 17)(18, 19, 21, 22, 23) skeins

NEEDLES

US 6 (4mm) 16" and 32" circular needles and set of DPNs, or size to obtain gauge

US 5 (3.75mm) 16" circular needles and set of DPNs, or one size smaller than size used to obtain gauge

NOTIONS

Yarn Needle
Stitch Markers
Stitch Holder or Scrap Yarn

GAUGE

22 sts and 34 rnds = 4" in Broken Rib Pattern in the round on larger needles, blocked

For pattern support, contact kristen@kristentendyke.com

Palora Pullover

Notes:

Simplicity and ease make this oversized, cozy pullover a great beginner sweater to knit. Working it top-down makes it easy to try on as it's being made and adjust the sleeve and body lengths as needed.

The Palora Pullover is worked seamlessly from the top down. The yoke is increased from the neck to the underarm, then the sleeves and body are divided and worked separately.

The back and front are split after the main body is worked, and the ribbing sections are worked separately, back and forth in rows.

3x3 Rib (in the round over a multiple of 6 sts)
Rnd 1: (K3, P3) to end.
Rep Rnd 1 for pattern.

3x3 Rib (flat over a multiple of 6 sts plus 3)
Row 1 (WS): Sl1 P-wise WYIF, P2, (K3, P3) to end.
Row 2 (RS): Sl1 K-wise WYIB, K2, (P3, K3) to end.
Rep Rows 1–2 for pattern.

Broken Ribbing (in the round over a multiple of 2 sts)
Rnd 1: (K1, P1) to end.
Rnd 2: K all.
Rep Rnds 1–2 for pattern.

DIRECTIONS

Yoke
With smaller 16″ circular needles, loosely CO 120 (132, 138, 144, 156)(162, 168, 174, 180, 180) sts. PM for BOR and join to work in the rnd, being careful not to twist sts.
Work 3x3 Rib for seven rnds.
Change to larger 16″ circular needles.

Sizes 37 (-, 44.25, 48, -)(55.25, 59, -, 65, 67.75)″ Only
Inc Rnd: *K30 (-, 69, 36, -)(81, 42, -, 90, 45), M1; rep from * around. 124 (-, 140, 148, -)(164, 172, -, 182, 184) sts.

Sizes - (40.75, -, -, 51.75)(-, -, 61.5, -, -)″ Only
Next Rnd: K all.

Resume All Sizes
Next Rnd: *P33 for sleeve, PM for raglan, P29 (33, 37, 41, 45)(49, 53, 54, 58, 59) for body, PM for raglan; rep from * once more.

Shape Raglan
Change to longer circular needles when sts no longer fit comfortably on shorter circular needles.
Rnd 1 (Inc): (K1, M1, K to 1 st before next M, M1, K1, SM) to end. 8 sts inc.
Rnd 2: *K1, (P1, K1) to M, SM; rep from * to end.
Rnd 3: Rep Rnd 1. 8 sts inc.
Rnd 4: *K2, (P1, K1) to 1 st before M, K1, SM; rep from * to end.

Rep Rnds 1–4 15 (16, 17, 18, 19)(20, 21, 22, 23, 24) more times, then rep Rnds 1–2 once. 388 (412, 436, 460, 484)(508, 532, 550, 574, 592) sts; 99 (103, 107, 111, 115)(119, 123, 127, 131, 135) sts each sleeve, 95 (103, 111, 119, 127)(135, 143, 148, 156, 161) sts each Back and Front.

Divide Body & Sleeves
Next Rnd: Remove M, place next 99 (103, 107, 111, 115)(119, 123, 127, 131, 135) sts onto st holder or scrap yarn for sleeve, remove M, use Backward Loop Cast On method to CO 4 (4, 6, 6, 8)(8, 10, 10, 12, 12) sts, PM for new BOR, CO another 3 (5, 5, 7, 7)(9, 9, 11, 11, 13) sts, K to next M, remove M, place next 99 (103, 107, 111, 115)(119, 123, 127, 131, 135) sts onto st holder or scrap yarn for sleeve, remove M, CO 7 (9, 11, 13, 15)(17, 19, 21, 23, 25) sts, remove M, K to end. 204 (224, 244, 264, 284)(304, 324, 338, 358, 372) sts.

Body
Cont working in Broken Ribbing as established until Body measures 9.5″ from underarm, ending after Rnd 2 of pattern.
Next Rnd: K all.

Sizes 37 (-, 44.25, 48, -)(55.25, 59, 61.5, -, 67.75)″ Only
Inc Rnd: *P34 (-, 122, 44, -)(152, 54, 84, -, 62), M1P; rep from * around. 210 (-, 246, 270, -)(306, 330, 342, -, 378) sts.

Sizes - (40.75, -, -, 51.75)(-, -, -, 65, -)″ Only
Dec Rnd: *P- (110, -, -, 140)(-, -, -, 89, -), P2tog; rep from * around. - (222, -, -, 282)(-, -, -, 354, -) sts.

Resume All Sizes
Next Rnd: K around.

Divide Back & Front
Next Rnd: Remove M, place next 105 (111, 123, 135, 141)(153, 165, 171, 177, 189) sts onto st holder or scrap yarn for Front. Cont working back and forth in rows on remaining 105 (111, 123, 135, 141)(153, 165, 171, 177, 189) sts for Back as follows.

Back
Beginning with a WS row, work 3x3 Rib for 6″, slipping first st of every row as described in 3x3 Rib flat directions, ending after a WS row.
BO all sts in pattern.

Front
Return 105 (111, 123, 135, 141)(153, 165, 171, 177, 189) held Front sts to larger needles and join yarn to work a WS row.
Work 3x3 Rib for 3″, slipping first st of every row, and ending after a WS row.
BO all sts in pattern.

Sleeves (make two the same)

Return 99 (103, 107, 111, 115)(119, 123, 127, 131, 135) held sts from one sleeve to larger 16″ circular needles.

Joining Rnd: Beginning at center of underarm, PU and K 3 (5, 5, 7, 7)(9, 9, 11, 11, 13) sts along underarm CO sts, K to end of held sts, then PU and K 4 (4, 6, 6, 8)(8, 10, 10, 12, 12) sts from remaining underarm CO sts. PM for BOR and join to work in the rnd. 106 (112, 118, 124, 130)(136, 142, 148, 154, 160) sts.

Shape Sleeve

Change to DPNs or use Magic Loop method when sts no longer fit comfortably on circular needles.

Work Broken Ribbing for three rnds.

Dec Rnd: K1, K2tog, K to last 2 sts, SSK. 2 sts dec.

Cont as established and rep Dec Rnd every four rnds 15 (12, 9, 9, 6)(3, 3, 0, 0, 0) more times, then every other rnd 16 (22, 28, 28, 34)(40, 40, 46, 46, 46) times. 42 (42, 42, 48, 48)(48, 54, 54, 60, 66) sts remain.

Next Rnd: K all.
Next Rnd: P all.
Next Rnd: K all.
Work 3x3 Rib for 3″.
BO all sts loosely in pattern.

Finishing

Weave in ends, wash, and block to diagram.

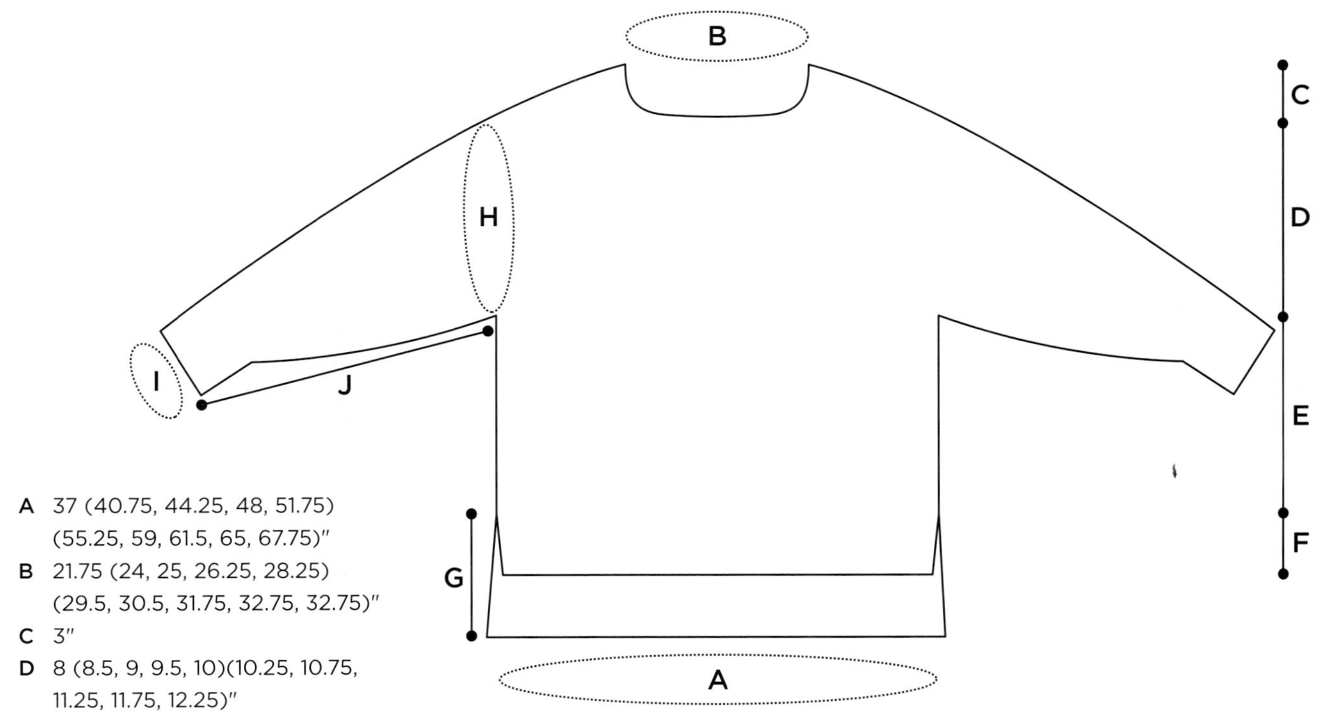

A 37 (40.75, 44.25, 48, 51.75)
(55.25, 59, 61.5, 65, 67.75)″

B 21.75 (24, 25, 26.25, 28.25)
(29.5, 30.5, 31.75, 32.75, 32.75)″

C 3″

D 8 (8.5, 9, 9.5, 10)(10.25, 10.75,
11.25, 11.75, 12.25)″

E 9.5″

F 3″

G 6″

H 19.25 (20.25, 21.5, 22.5, 23.75)
(24.75, 25.75, 27, 28, 29)″

I 7.75 (7.75, 7.75, 8.75, 8.75)
(8.75, 9.75, 9.75, 11, 12)″

J 15″

PROTEA SWEATER

by Sierra Morningstar

FINISHED MEASUREMENTS

33 (36.5, 40, 43.5, 47, 50.75)(54.25, 57.5, 61.25, 65.75, 69.25)" finished bust circumference; meant to be worn with approx 6" positive ease
Sample is 40" size; model is 33.5" bust

YARN

Wool of the Andes™ (worsted weight, 100% Peruvian Highland Wool; 110 yards/50g): Brass Heather 25638 10 (11, 12, 13, 14, 15)(16, 17, 18, 20, 21) skeins

NEEDLES

US 8 (5mm) DPNs and 24–48" circular needles (long enough to hold full body stitches), or size to obtain gauge
US 7 (4.5mm) 16" circular needles, or size to obtain gauge

NOTIONS

Yarn Needle
2 Stitch Markers
4 Removable Stitch Markers or Safety Pins
Stitch Holders or Scrap Yarn

GAUGE

18 sts and 34 rows = 4" in Garter Stitch on larger needles, blocked
18 sts and 34 rows/rnds = 4" in 2x2 Garter Rib worked flat and in the round on larger needles, blocked (rounds gauge is not critical)
21 sts and 34 rnds = 4" in 2x2 Rib in the round on smaller needles, blocked (rounds gauge is not critical)

For pattern support, contact Morn5420@yahoo.com

Protea Sweater

Notes:

This simple but interesting sweater takes its name from Proteus, the Greek god of rivers. An unbroken Garter Rib flows down the length of the arm, from saddle shoulder to cuff, like a river's current, while the Garter Stitch body resembles little ripples at the water's surface.

Protea is worked flat from the top down, beginning with saddle shoulders and ending above the bottom ribbing. The sleeves are picked up from the body and worked flat to above the cuff. The sides and sleeves are then seamed, and the bottom ribbing and cuffs are worked in the round.

A Stockinette selvage stitch is worked on each side of the body for the length of the armhole to facilitate picking up the sleeve stitches. These stitches are decreased after the armhole and the remainder of the body is worked without the selvage stitch.

2x2 Garter Rib (flat over a multiple of 4 sts plus 2)
Row 1 (RS): K across.
Row 2 (WS): P2, (K2, P2) to end.
Rep Rows 1–2 for pattern.

2x2 Garter Rib (in the round over a multiple of 4 sts)
Rnd 1: K around.
Rnd 2: (K2, P2) to end of rnd.
Rep Rnds 1–2 for pattern.

2x2 Rib (in the round over a multiple of 4 sts)
Rnd 1: (P2, K2) to end of rnd.
Rep Rnd 1 for pattern.

DIRECTIONS

Saddle Shoulders (make two the same)
Using Long Tail Cast On and larger needles, CO 20 sts.
Setup Row (WS): P1, PM, P2, (K2, P2) to last st, PM, P1.
Row 1 (RS): K1, SM, work 2x2 Garter Rib to M, SM, K1.
Row 2 (WS): P1, SM, work 2x2 Garter Rib to M, SM, P1.
Rep Rows 1–2 until piece measures 5.5 (6.5, 7, 7.75, 8.75, 9)(10, 11, 11.25, 12.25, 13.5)", ending with a WS row and removing Ms. Place sts on st holder or scrap yarn.

Back
Using larger needles, CO 1 st; beginning at end of saddle shoulder with live sts, with RS facing, PU and K 25 (29, 31, 35, 39, 41)(45, 49, 51, 55, 59) sts along entire long edge, using Cabled Cast On, CO 26 (26, 30, 30, 30, 34)(34, 34, 38, 40, 40) sts; beginning at CO end of second saddle shoulder, with RS facing, PU and K 25 (29, 31, 35, 39, 41)(45, 49, 51, 55, 59) sts along entire long edge, CO 1 st. 78 (86, 94, 102, 110, 118)(126, 134, 142, 152, 160) sts.

Setup Row (WS): P1, PM, K to last st, PM, P1.
Row 1 (RS): K across.
Row 2 (WS): P1, SM, K to M, SM, P1.
Rep Rows 1–2 for 4.5 (5, 5.5, 6, 6.5, 7)(7.5, 7.75, 8.25, 8.5, 9)" maintaining selvage st on each edge, ending with a WS row.

Place removable M on each side.

Next Row: SSK, K to last 2 sts, K2tog. 76 (84, 92, 100, 108, 116)(124, 132, 140, 150, 158) sts.
Cont Garter Stitch, without selvage sts, until piece measures 18 (18.5, 19, 19.5, 20, 20.5)(20.75, 21, 21.25, 21.5, 21.75)" from edge of saddle shoulder, ending with a WS row.
Place sts on st holder or scrap yarn.

Front
Left Front
Starting at CO end of saddle shoulder, with RS facing and using larger needles, PU 25 (29, 31, 35, 39, 41)(45, 49, 51, 55, 59) sts along long edge, CO 1 st. 26 (30, 32, 36, 40, 42)(46, 50, 52, 56, 60) sts.
Setup Row (WS): P1, PM, K to last st, P1.
Row 1 (RS): KFB, K to end. 1 st inc.
Row 2 (WS): P1, SM, K to last st, P1.
Rep Rows 1–2 7 (7, 9, 9, 9, 10)(10, 10, 11, 12, 12) more times. 34 (38, 42, 46, 50, 53)(57, 61, 64, 69, 73) sts. Place sts on st holder or scrap yarn. Break yarn.

Right Front
Starting at end of saddle shoulder with live sts, with RS facing, CO 1, PU 25 (29, 31, 35, 39, 41)(45, 49, 51, 55, 59) sts along long edge. 26 (30, 32, 36, 40, 42)(46, 50, 52, 56, 60) sts.
Setup Row (WS): P1, K to last st, PM, P1.
Row 1 (RS): K to last st, KFB. 1 st inc.
Row 2 (WS): P1, K to M, SM, P1.
Rep Rows 1–2 7 (7, 9, 9, 9, 10)(10, 10, 11, 12, 12) more times. 34 (38, 42, 46, 50, 53)(57, 61, 64, 69, 73) sts.

Join Front
Next Row (RS): K across Right Front, CO 10 (10, 10, 10, 10, 12)(12, 12, 14, 14, 14) sts, K across held Left Front sts. 78 (86, 94, 102, 110, 118)(126, 134, 142, 152, 160) sts.
Work Garter Stitch with 1 St st selvage st on each side, as for the back, until piece measures 4.5 (5, 5.5, 6, 6.5, 7)(7.5, 7.75, 8.25, 8.5, 9)" from saddle shoulders, ending with a WS row. Place removable M on each side.

Next Row: SSK, K to last 2 sts, K2tog. 76 (84, 92, 100, 108, 116)(124, 132, 140, 150, 158) sts.
Cont Garter Stitch, without selvage sts, until piece measures 18 (18.5, 19, 19.5, 20, 20.5)(20.75, 21, 21.25, 21.5, 21.75)" from edge of saddle shoulder, ending with a WS row.

Sleeves (make two the same)
Place 20 held live saddle sts onto larger needles. With RS facing, starting at removable M, PU and K 19 (22, 24, 26, 28, 30)(33, 34, 36, 38, 40) sts, K1 from saddle, PM, K18 across saddle to last st, PM, K1, PU and K 19 (22, 24, 26, 28, 30)(33, 34, 36, 38, 40) sts. 58 (64, 68, 72, 76, 80)(86, 88, 92, 96, 100) sts.

Work Garter Stitch with 2x2 Garter Rib between Ms as established for 1", ending on a WS row.

Dec Row (RS): K1, K2tog, work as established to last 3 sts, SSK, K1. 2 sts dec.

Cont as established and rep Dec Row every 12 (8, 8, 8, 8, 6)(6, 6, 6, 4, 4) rows 5 (2, 12, 2, 12, 6)(2, 4, 12, 1, 7) more times, then every 14 (10, 10, 10, 10, 8)(8, 8, 8, 6, 6) rows 3 (9, 1, 9, 1, 9)(12, 11, 5, 18, 14) times. 40 (40, 40, 48, 48, 48)(56, 56, 56, 56, 56) sts.

WE as established until sleeve measures 14.5 (14.5, 14.5, 14.5, 14.5, 14.5)(15, 15, 15, 15, 15)" from PU edge. Place sts on st holder or scrap yarn.

Finishing

Body

Sew side seams.

Place held body sts back onto larger circular needles. PM for BOR—it does not matter which side of body M is placed. 152 (168, 184, 200, 216, 232)(248, 264, 280, 300, 316) sts.

Work 2x2 Garter Rib in the rnd for 2.5".

BO all sts.

Sleeves

Sew underarm seams.

Place held sleeve sts onto larger DPNs. PM for BOR.

Work 2x2 Garter Rib as follows.

Rnd 1: K all.

Rnd 2: K1, P2, (K2, P2) to last st, K1.

Rep Rnds 1–2 until cuff measures 2.5".

BO all sts.

Rep for second sleeve.

Neckband

Using smaller needle and starting at back neck, below right saddle shoulder, PU and K: 26 (26, 30, 30, 30, 34)(34, 34, 38, 40, 40) sts from back neck, 18 sts from left saddle shoulder, 12 (12, 14, 14, 14, 15)(15, 15, 16, 17, 17) sts from left front, 10 (10, 10, 10, 10, 12)(12, 12, 14, 14, 14) sts from bottom front, 12 (12, 14, 14, 14, 15)(15, 15, 16, 17, 17) sts from right front, 18 sts from right saddle shoulder. 96 (96, 104, 104, 104, 112)(112, 112, 120, 124, 124) sts.

PM and join for knitting in the rnd.

Beginning with P2, work 2x2 Rib (not Garter Rib) for 1".

BO loosely.

Weave in ends, wash, and block to diagram.

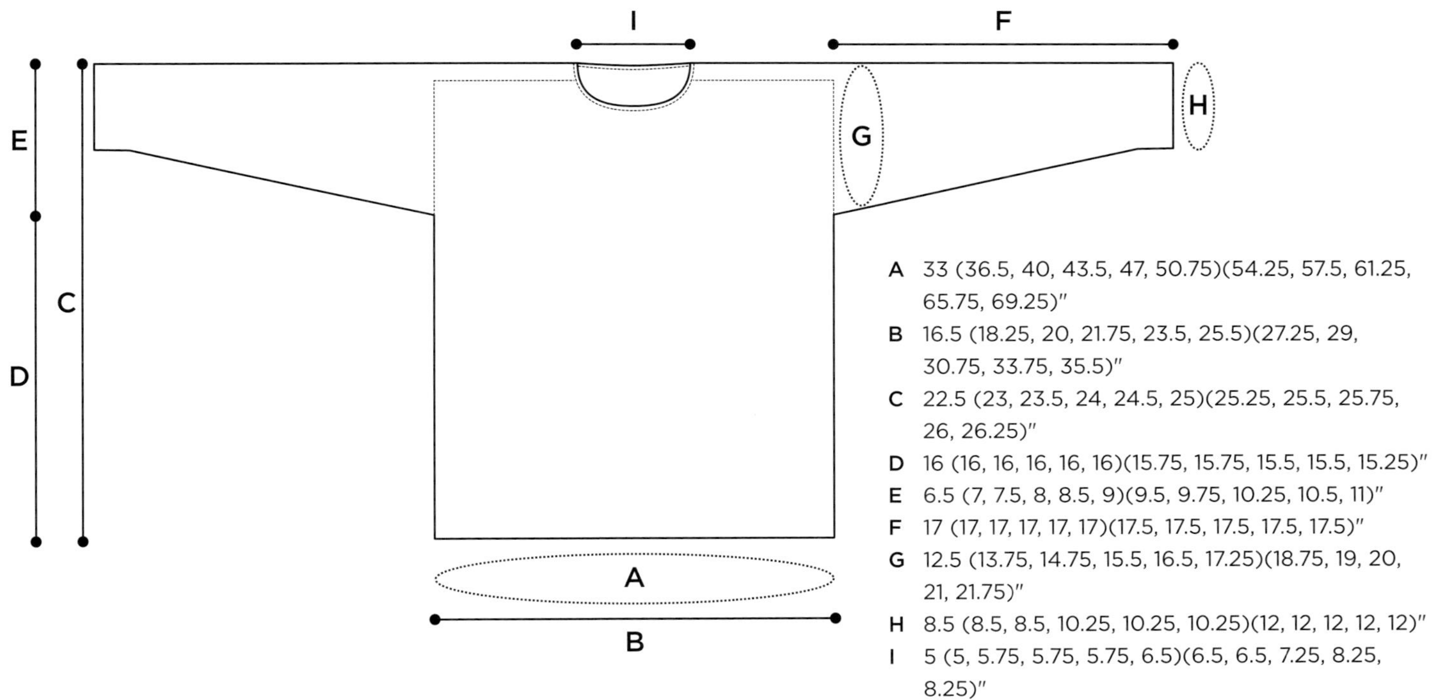

A 33 (36.5, 40, 43.5, 47, 50.75)(54.25, 57.5, 61.25, 65.75, 69.25)"

B 16.5 (18.25, 20, 21.75, 23.5, 25.5)(27.25, 29, 30.75, 33.75, 35.5)"

C 22.5 (23, 23.5, 24, 24.5, 25)(25.25, 25.5, 25.75, 26, 26.25)"

D 16 (16, 16, 16, 16, 16)(15.75, 15.75, 15.5, 15.5, 15.25)"

E 6.5 (7, 7.5, 8, 8.5, 9)(9.5, 9.75, 10.25, 10.5, 11)"

F 17 (17, 17, 17, 17, 17)(17.5, 17.5, 17.5, 17.5, 17.5)"

G 12.5 (13.75, 14.75, 15.5, 16.5, 17.25)(18.75, 19, 20, 21, 21.75)"

H 8.5 (8.5, 8.5, 10.25, 10.25, 10.25)(12, 12, 12, 12, 12)"

I 5 (5, 5.75, 5.75, 5.75, 6.5)(6.5, 6.5, 7.25, 8.25, 8.25)"

TEXTURED DIAMONDS PULLOVER

by Jodi Lemieux

FINISHED MEASUREMENTS

37 (40.5, 43.75, 47.25, 50.5)(54, 57.25, 60.75, 64, 67.5)" finished bust circumference; meant to be worn with 4–6" positive ease
Sample is 40.5" size; model is 33.5" bust

YARN

Twill™ (worsted weight, 100% Superwash Merino Wool; 149 yards/100g): Bare 27844, 9 (10, 11, 12, 13)(14, 15, 16, 17, 19) hanks

NEEDLES

US 8 (5mm) straight or circular needles (24" or longer), or size to obtain gauge

US 6 (4mm) 16" circular needles or DPNs, or two sizes smaller than size used to obtain gauge
US 8 (5mm) DPN or straight or circular needle for 3-Needle Bind Off

NOTIONS

Yarn Needle
Stitch Markers
Removable Stitch Markers or Safety Pins
Stitch Holder or Scrap Yarn

GAUGE

19 sts and 30 rows = 4" in Diamond Pattern on larger needles, blocked

For pattern support, contact jmlem511@gmail.com

Textured Diamonds Pullover

Notes:

Diamonds are a girl's best friend! Strategically placed purl stitches against a stockinette stitch background form a diamond lattice pattern reminiscent of embossed brocade fabric.

The Textured Diamonds Pullover is worked flat from the bottom up and then seamed. The shoulders are joined with a 3-Needle Bind Off. To provide a more refined fit to the modified drop shoulder styling, stitches are decreased rapidly over several rows rather than bound off in one step.

When shaping the armholes, neck edges, and sleeves, it may be useful to use stitch markers to outline the first and last full pattern repeats.

Chart is worked flat; read RS rows (odd numbers) from right to left, and WS rows (even numbers) from left to right.

When shaping in pattern, maintain two selvage stitches in Stockinette Stitch at beginning and end of row. Work partial charts at beginning and/or end of row as needed.

Diamonds (flat over a multiple of 8 sts plus 2)
Row 1 (RS): K1, (K4, P1, K3) to last st, K1.
Row 2 (WS): P1, (P2, K1, P1, K1, P3) to last st, P1.
Row 3: K1, (K2, P1, K3, P1, K1) to last st, K1.
Row 4: P1, (K1, P5, K1, P1) to last st, P1.
Row 5: K1, (P1, K7) to last st, P1.
Row 6: Rep Row 4.
Row 7: Rep Row 3.
Row 8: Rep Row 2.
Rep Rows 1–8 for pattern.

DIRECTIONS

Back
Using larger needles, CO 90 (98, 106, 114, 122)(130, 138, 146, 154, 162) sts using the Long Tail Cast On method.
Noting that first row is a WS row, purl three rows.
Work 2x2 Rib until piece measures 3″ from CO edge, ending with a WS row.
Begin working Diamonds pattern and rep Rows 1–8 until piece measures 18″ from CO edge, ending with Row 8.
Mark beginning and end of next row with removable Ms or safety pins.

Shape Armholes
Dec Row 1 (RS): K1, SSK, work Diamonds as established to last 3 sts, K2tog, K1. 2 sts dec.
Dec Row 2 (WS): P1, P2tog, work Diamonds as established to last 3 sts, P2tog TBL, P1. 2 sts dec.
Rep Dec Rows 1–2 2 (2, 2, 2, 2)(5, 6, 6, 7, 7) more times, then rep Dec Row 1 every RS row 6 (8, 9, 11, 12)(10, 11, 14, 15, 17) times. 66 (70, 76, 80, 86)(86, 88, 90, 92, 96) sts.
WE in Diamonds pattern as established until piece measures 8.5 (9, 9.5, 10, 10.5)(10.5, 10.75, 10.75, 11, 11.5)″ above M, ending with a WS row.

Next Row (RS): Work 13 (14, 17, 18, 20)(20, 20, 21, 21, 23) sts in pattern, then place them on st holder or scrap yarn; BO next 40 (42, 42, 44, 46)(46, 48, 48, 50, 50) sts, work 13 (14, 17, 18, 20)(20, 20, 21, 21, 23) remaining sts and place them on st holder or scrap yarn. Make a note of ending chart row to match Back to Front.

Front
Work as for Back until armholes measure 4 (4.5, 5, 5.5, 6)(6, 6.25, 6.25, 6.5, 7)″ above Ms, ending with a WS row. 66 (70, 76, 80, 86)(86, 88, 90, 92, 96) sts.

Shape Left Side Neck
Make a note of first chart row worked on LH side neck shaping in order to match pattern on RH side. Mark center 12 (14, 14, 16, 18)(18, 20, 20, 22, 22) sts with removable Ms. 27 (28, 31, 32, 34)(34, 34, 35, 35, 37) sts each side of Ms for shoulders.
Cont working Diamonds pattern as established and at the same time, with RS facing, shape LH side of neck as follows.
Row 1 (RS): Work in pattern to 3 sts before first M, K2tog, K1. 1 st dec. Place center 12 (14, 14, 16, 18)(18, 20, 20, 22, 22) sts on st holder or scrap yarn, removing Ms. Turn.
Row 2 (WS): Work in pattern to end.
Rep Rows 1–2 thirteen more times. 13 (14, 17, 18, 20)(20, 20, 21, 21, 23) sts remain for LH shoulder.
WE in pattern until armhole measures 8.5 (9, 9.5, 10, 10.5)(10.5, 10.75, 10.75, 11, 11.5)″ above M, ending after a RS row. Break yarn and place 13 (14, 17, 18, 20)(20, 20, 21, 21, 23) sts on st holder or scrap yarn.

Shape Right Side Neck
With RS facing, rejoin yarn and cont working Diamonds as established, and at the same time, shape RH side of neck as follows.
Row 1 (RS): K1, SSK, work in pattern to end. 1 st dec.
Row 2 (WS): Work in pattern to end.
Rep Rows 1–2 thirteen more times. 13 (14, 17, 18, 20)(20, 20, 21, 21, 23) sts remain for RH shoulder.
WE in pattern until armhole measures 8.5 (9, 9.5, 10, 10.5)(10.5, 10.75, 10.75, 11, 11.5)″ above M, ending after a RS row. Break yarn and place 13 (14, 17, 18, 20)(20, 20, 21, 21, 23) sts on st holder or scrap yarn.

Sleeves (make two the same)
Using larger needles, CO 42 (42, 42, 50, 50)(50, 58, 58, 58, 64) sts using the Long Tail Cast On method.
Noting that first row is a WS row, purl three rows.
Work 2x2 Rib until piece measures 3″ from CO edge, ending with a WS row.

Shape Sleeve
In this section incs and patterning are worked at the same time. Work inc sts into established Diamonds pattern.
Beginning with Row 1, work four rows in Diamonds pattern.

Inc Row (RS): K1, M1R, work in pattern to last st, M1L, K1.
2 sts inc.

Working in pattern as established, rep Inc Row every four rows 2 (11, 17, 14, 20)(23, 14, 17, 17, 17) more times, then every six rows 16 (10, 6, 8, 4)(2, 8, 6, 6, 4) times. 80 (86, 90, 96, 100)(102, 104, 106, 106, 108) sts.

Cont in pattern as established until piece measures 18″ from CO edge, ending with Row 8. Mark beginning and end of next row with removable Ms or safety pins.

Shape Cap

Dec Row 1 (RS): K1, SSK, work in pattern to last 3 sts, K2tog, K1. 2 sts dec.

Dec Row 2 (WS): P1, P2tog, work in pattern to last 3 sts, P2tog TBL, P1. 2 sts dec.

Rep Dec Rows 1–2 2 (2, 2, 2, 2)(5, 6, 6, 7, 7) more times, then rep Dec Row 1 every RS row 6 (8, 9, 11, 12)(10, 11, 14, 15, 17) times. 56 (58, 60, 62, 64)(58, 54, 50, 44, 42) sts. BO all sts on next RS row.

Shoulders

With RS of front facing, place LH side 13 (14, 17, 18, 20)(20, 20, 21, 21, 23) shoulder sts on needle. With WS of back facing, place LH side 13 (14, 17, 18, 20)(20, 20, 21, 21, 23) shoulder sts on second needle. With RSs facing tog, seam with 3-Needle Bind Off.

Rep for RH side shoulder.

Neckband

With smaller circular needle or DPNs and RS facing, beginning at RH back shoulder, PU and K 40 (42, 42, 44, 46)(46, 48, 48, 50, 50) sts along back neck, PU and K 26 sts along LH side of front neck, K12 (14, 14, 16, 18)(18, 20, 20, 22, 22) sts from front neck holder, PU and K 26 sts along RH side of front neck. 104 (108, 108, 112, 116)(116, 120, 120, 124, 124) sts.

PM and join to work in the rnd.
Purl one rnd.
Work 2x2 Rib for six rnds.
BO loosely in pattern.

Finishing

Using Mattress Stitch, attach sleeves to body matching shaped edges above Ms to form angled armholes.
Using Mattress Stitch, join side and sleeve seams.
Weave in ends, wash, and block to diagram.

LEGEND

K
RS: Knit stitch
WS: Purl stitch

P
RS: Purl stitch
WS: Knit stitch

Pattern Repeat

Diamonds

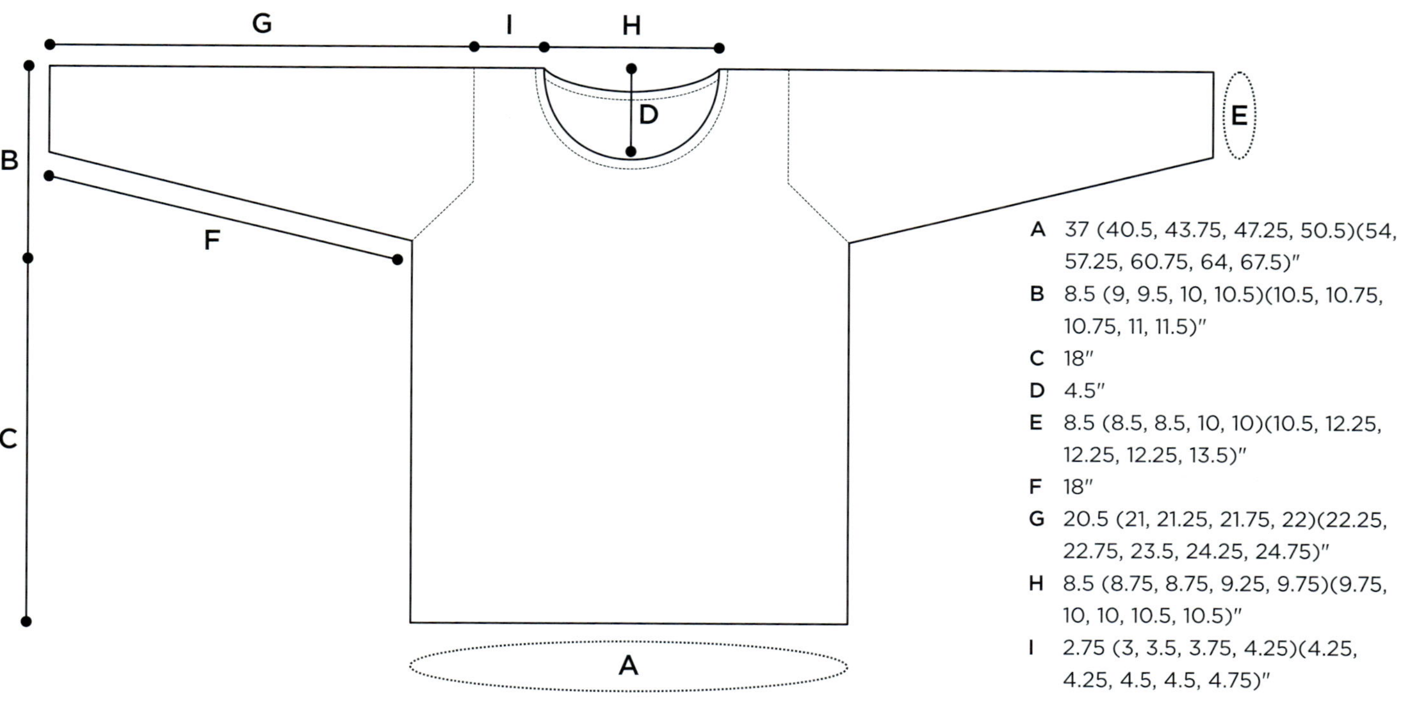

A 37 (40.5, 43.75, 47.25, 50.5)(54, 57.25, 60.75, 64, 67.5)″

B 8.5 (9, 9.5, 10, 10.5)(10.5, 10.75, 10.75, 11, 11.5)″

C 18″

D 4.5″

E 8.5 (8.5, 8.5, 10, 10)(10.5, 12.25, 12.25, 12.25, 13.5)″

F 18″

G 20.5 (21, 21.25, 21.75, 22)(22.25, 22.75, 23.5, 24.25, 24.75)″

H 8.5 (8.75, 8.75, 9.25, 9.75)(9.75, 10, 10, 10.5, 10.5)″

I 2.75 (3, 3.5, 3.75, 4.25)(4.25, 4.25, 4.5, 4.5, 4.75)″

TOAST BEANIE

by Violet LeBeaux

FINISHED MEASUREMENTS

20″ brim circumference × 8.5 (10.5)″ height, not including pom-pom

YARN

Swish™ (worsted weight, 100% Fine Superwash Merino Wool; 110 yards/50g): C1 Dove Heather 25631, 2 skeins; C2 Lost Lake Heather 25146, 1 skein

NEEDLES

US 6 (4mm) DPNs and 16″ circular needles or 24″ or longer circular needles for Magic Loop technique, or size to obtain gauge

NOTIONS

Yarn Needle
Stitch Marker
12cm Faux Fur Pom-Pom (optional)

GAUGE

20 sts and 40 rnds = 4″ in Waffle Stitch in the round, blocked (note that this is approximate due to amount of stretch in the ribbing)

For pattern support, contact violetlebeaux@gmail.com

Toast Beanie

Notes:

Toast is an ultimate winter favorite. It features a versatile textured waffle design that suits all styles. The colored stripes and fluffy pom-pom make a fashionable gifting choice, and the stretchiness means it's perfect for recipients whose sizing is not certain!

Construction is bottom up in the round, beginning with a rib that transitions into the waffle texture. The stripes continue all the way up through the decreases to create a striking effect. Sizing for beanie and slouch lengths are included.

Garter Waffle Stitch (in the round over a multiple of 4 sts)
Rnd 1: K all.
Rnd 2: K1, P3.
Rnds 3–8: Rep Rnds 1–2 three more times.
Rnds 9–10: K all.
Rep Rnds 1–10 for pattern.

DIRECTIONS

Brim

With C1, loosely CO 100 sts (or a multiple of 4 sts).
Join to work in the rnd, being careful not to twist sts, and PM for BOR.

Work 2x2 Rib for 1".
Next Rnd: (SSK, M1P, P2) to end.

Body

With C1, work Garter Waffle Stitch Rnds 1–10 2 (4) times, then Rnds 1–8 once.
With C2, work Garter Waffle Stitch Rnds 9–10, then Rnds 1–10.
With C1, work Garter Waffle Stitch Rnds 1–8.
With C2, work Garter Waffle Stitch Rnds 9–10 then 1–8.

Crown

Rnd 1: With C2, (K2, K2tog) to end. 75 sts.
Rnd 2: With C2, K all.
Rnd 3: With C1, K all.
Rnd 4: With C1, (K1, P2) to end.
Rnds 5–10: Rep Rnds 3–4 three more times. Break C1.
Rnd 11: With C2, (K1, K2tog) to end. 50 sts.
Rnds 12–13: K all.
Rnd 14: (SSK) to end. 25 sts.
Rnd 15–16: K all.
BO by passing yarn through remaining sts and pulling tightly.

Finishing

Optionally, attach pom-pom to top of hat.
Weave in ends, wash, and block to measurements.

VIRAGO VEST

by Sierra Morningstar

FINISHED MEASUREMENTS

32 (36, 40, 44, 48)(52, 56, 60, 64)″
finished bust and hip circumference;
meant to be worn with 2–4″ positive ease
(height of bottom slits can be adjusted
to provide more ease if desired)
Sample is 36″ size; model is 33.5″ bust

YARN

Simply Wool™ (worsted weight, 100%
Eco Wool; 218 yards/100g): Wanda
27468, 4 (4, 5, 5, 6)(6, 7, 7, 8) hanks

NEEDLES

US 8 (5mm) 16″ and 24″ circular needles,
or size to obtain gauge

US 8 (5mm) DPN or straight or circular
needle for 3-Needle Bind Off
US 9 (5.5mm) 16″ circular needles, or one
size larger than size used to obtain gauge

NOTIONS

Yarn Needle
2 Stitch Markers
Stitch Holders or Scrap Yarn

GAUGE

18 sts and 30 rows = 4″ in Chevron
Pattern, blocked
18 sts and 30 rows = 4″ in Garter Stitch,
blocked

For pattern support, contact Morn5420@yahoo.com

Virago Vest

Notes:

Historically, the word virago meant a noble female warrior of strength and spirit. Today, this striking, streamlined tunic is the perfect armor for modern-day warriors as they set out to conquer the world!

Virago is knit in pieces and seamed. The bottom of the vest has a 6″ split to help accommodate the hips. If a longer split is desired, simply begin seaming pieces together farther up from the bottom.

Chevron Pattern (flat over a multiple of 18 sts plus 1)
Row 1 (RS): K1 *(P1, K2, P1) two times, K1; rep from * to end of row.
Row 2 (WS): P1, *P2, (K2, P2, K2, P1) two times, P2; rep from * to end of row.
Row 3: *(K2, P2) two times, K1; rep from * to last st, K1.
Row 4: *P1, (K2, P2) two times, P1, (P2, K2) two times; rep from * to last st, P1.
Rep Rows 1–4 for pattern.
Sizes 32 (-, 40, -, 48)(-, 56, -, 64)″ will call for an additional half-rep of st pattern on WS rows. When knitting the back, this half-rep is at the beginning of the row; when knitting the front, it is at the end. Please note special instructions within pattern for these sizes.

DIRECTIONS

Back
Using Long Tail Cast On method and smaller needles, CO 74 (83, 92, 101, 110)(119, 128, 137, 146) sts.
Setup Row (WS): Sl1 WYIB, K4, PM, K to last 5 sts, PM, K to end.
Rows 1–4: Sl1 WYIB, K to end.

Begin Chevron Pattern
Row 1 (RS): Sl1 WYIB, K4, SM, work Chevron Pattern to M, SM, K to end.
Row 2 (WS): Sl1 WYIB, K4, SM, work Chevron Pattern to M, SM, K to end. **For Sizes 32 (-, 40, -, 48)(-, 56, -, 64)″** work first 9 sts of Chevron Pattern on Row 2 as: P1, K2, P2, K2, P2.
Row 3: Sl1 WYIB, K4, SM, work Chevron Pattern to M, SM, K to end.
Row 4: Sl1 WYIB, K4, SM, work Chevron Pattern to M, SM, K to end. **For Sizes 32 (-, 40, -, 48)(-, 56, -, 64)″** work first 9 sts of Chevron Pattern on Row 4 as: P3, K2, P2, K2.
WE as established until piece measures 18″ from CO edge, ending with a WS row.

Shape Armhole
BO 5 (6, 7, 7, 8)(9, 10, 11, 12) sts at beginning of next two rows, then 0 (2, 3, 6, 8)(9, 10, 10, 11) sts at beginning of following two rows. 64 (67, 72, 75, 78)(83, 88, 95, 100) sts.
Dec Row (RS): K1, K2tog, work Chevron Pattern as established to last 3 sts, SSK, K1. 2 sts dec.

Next Row (WS): P2, work Chevron Pattern as established to last 2 sts, P2.
Rep Dec Row every RS row 2 (2, 3, 4, 4)(5, 7, 8, 9) more times. 58 (61, 64, 65, 68)(71, 72, 77, 80) sts.

Keeping first and last 2 sts of every row in St st, cont in pattern until armhole measures 6.75 (7, 7.5, 8, 8.5)(9, 9.5, 10, 10.5)″ from underarm BO, ending with a RS row.
Next Row (WS): Work 13 (14, 15, 15, 16)(17, 17, 18, 19) sts, BO 32 (33, 34, 35, 36)(37, 38, 41, 42) sts, work to end. Place live sts on st holders or scrap yarn.

Front
Using Long Tail Cast On method and smaller needles, CO 74 (83, 92, 101, 110)(119, 128, 137, 146) sts.
Setup Row (WS): Sl1 WYIB, K4, PM, K to last 5 sts, PM, K to end.
Rows 1–4: Sl1 WYIB, K to end.

Begin Chevron Pattern
Row 1 (RS): Sl1 WYIB, K4, SM, work Chevron Pattern to M, SM, K to end.
Row 2 (WS): Sl1 WYIB, K4, SM, work Chevron Pattern to M, SM, K to end. **For Sizes 32 (-, 40, -, 48)(-, 56, -, 64)″** work last 9 sts of Chevron Pattern on Row 2 as: P2, K2, P2, K2, P1.
Row 3: Sl1 WYIB, K4, SM, work Chevron Pattern to M, SM, K to end.
Row 4: Sl1 WYIB, K4, SM, work Chevron Pattern to M, SM, K to end. **For Sizes 32 (-, 40, -, 48)(-, 56, -, 64)″** work last 9 sts of Chevron Pattern on Row 4 as: K2, P2, K2, P3.
WE as established until piece measures 18″ from CO edge, ending with a WS row.

Shape Armhole
Work armhole shaping as for the Back. 58 (61, 64, 65, 68)(71, 72, 77, 80) sts.
WE until armhole measures 4 (4.25, 4.75, 5, 5.25)(5.75, 6.25, 6.5, 7)″ ending with a WS row.

Shape Neck
Next Row (RS): Work across 23 (24, 25, 25, 27)(28, 28, 30, 31) sts. Join a second ball of yarn and BO 12 (13, 14, 15, 14)(15, 16, 17, 18) sts, work to end.

Right Front
Next Row (WS): WE as established.
Cont as established and BO 2 sts at beginning of next three RS rows. 17 (18, 19, 19, 21)(22, 22, 24, 25) sts.
Next Row (WS): WE as established.
Dec Row (RS): SSK, work to end. 1 st dec.
Rep Dec Row every RS row 3 (3, 3, 3, 4)(4, 4, 5, 5) more times. 13 (14, 15, 15, 16)(17, 17, 18, 19) sts.
WE for seven rows, ending with a WS row.
Place sts on st holder or scrap yarn.

Left Front

Beginning with a WS row, using original ball of yarn, cont as established and BO 2 sts at beginning of next three WS rows. 17 (18, 19, 19, 21)(22, 22, 24, 25) sts.

Next Row (RS): WE as established.

Dec Row (WS): P2tog, work to end. 1 st dec.

Rep Dec Row every WS row 3 (3, 3, 3, 4)(4, 4, 5, 5) more times. 13 (14, 15, 15, 16)(17, 17, 18, 19) sts.

WE for eight rows, ending on a WS row.

Place sts on st holder or scrap yarn.

Finishing

Weave in ends, wash, and block to diagram measurements. With RSs facing, using 3-Needle Bind Off, seam shoulders tog. Beginning 6" up from hem, sew side seams. Adjust height of side slit if desired by beginning to sew seam higher up the side.

Armholes (make two the same)

Starting at center underarm, PU and K: 5 (6, 7, 7, 8)(9, 11, 11, 12) sts from underarm BO, 4 (4, 6, 7, 7)(8, 11, 12, 14) sts from underarm shaping, 25 (26, 27, 28, 30)(31, 31, 32, 32) sts from side of armhole to shoulder, 25 (26, 27, 28, 30)(31, 31, 32, 32) sts from side of armhole to beginning of underarm shaping, 4 (4, 6, 7, 7)(8, 11, 12, 14) sts from underarm shaping, 5 (6, 7, 7, 8)(9, 11, 11, 12) sts from underarm BO. 68 (72, 80, 84, 90)(96, 106, 110, 116) sts. PM and join for knitting in the rnd.

Purl one rnd.

Work Garter Stitch for two rnds.

BO all sts.

Turtleneck

Starting at shoulder seam and using smaller needles, PU and K: 32 (33, 34, 35, 36)(37, 38, 41, 42) sts from back neck, 15 (15, 15, 15, 17)(17, 17, 19, 19) sts from left front, 12 (13, 14, 15, 14)(15, 16, 17, 18) sts from base of neck, 15 (15, 15, 15, 17)(17, 17, 19, 19) sts from right front. 74 (76, 78, 80, 84)(86, 88, 96, 98) sts. PM and join for knitting in the rnd.

Purl one rnd.

Work Garter Stitch for 3.5".

Change to larger needles. Cont Garter Stitch until turtleneck measures 7".

BO all sts.

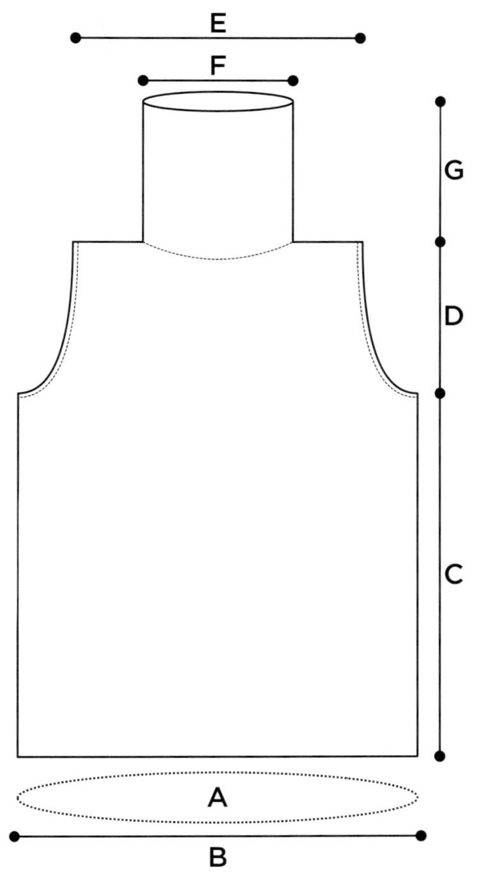

A 32 (36, 40, 44, 48)(52, 56, 60, 64)"

B 16.5 (18.5, 20.5, 22.5, 24.5)(26.5, 28.5, 30.5, 32.5)" (including seaming sts)

C 18"

D 6.75 (7, 7.5, 8, 8.5)(9, 9.5, 10, 10.5)"

E 13 (13.5, 14.25, 14.5, 15)(15.75, 16, 17, 17.75)"

F 7 (7.25, 7.5, 7.75, 8)(8.25, 8.5, 9, 9.25)"

G 7"

WAFFLE STITCH PULLOVER

by Emily Ringelman

FINISHED MEASUREMENTS

34 (38, 42, 46)(50, 54, 58, 62)" finished bust circumference; meant to be worn with 4-6" positive ease
Sample is 42" size; model is 33.5" bust

YARN

Swish™ (DK weight, 100% Fine Superwash Merino Wool; 123 yards/50g): Lost Lake Heather 25583, 9 (10, 11, 13) (14, 15, 17, 18) skeins

NEEDLES

US 6 (4mm) 16" and 24–32" circular needles, or size to obtain gauge
US 6 (4mm) DPNs or two 24" circular needles for two circulars technique or 32" or longer circular needles for Magic Loop technique, or size to obtain gauge

US 5 (3.75mm) 16" and 24–32" circular needles, or one size smaller than size used to obtain gauge
US 5 (3.75mm) DPNs or two 24" circular needles for two circulars technique or 32" or longer circular needles for Magic Loop technique, or one size smaller than size used to obtain gauge

NOTIONS

Yarn Needle
Stitch Markers
Stitch Holders or Scrap Yarn

GAUGE

24 sts and 32 rnds = 4" in Waffle Stitch Pattern in the round on larger needles, blocked

For pattern support, contact emily.ringelman@gmail.com

Waffle Stitch Pullover

Notes:

Reminiscent of a thermal under layer, the Waffle Stitch Pullover is a great everyday sweater. Plenty of positive ease makes it easy to wear and layer, and the easily memorized Waffle Stitch pattern makes for a rhythmic and soothing knit.

This sweater is worked from the bottom up in the round to the underarms, then split and worked flat for the front and back. The sleeves are worked from stitches picked up around the armholes. The sleeve and body lengths are easily customizable.

Waffle Stitch (flat over a multiple of 4 sts)
Row 1 (RS): (K2, P2) to end.
Row 2 (WS): (K2, P2) to end.
Rows 3–4: K across.
Rep Rows 1–4 for pattern.

Waffle Stitch (in the round over a multiple of 4 sts)
Rnds 1–2: (K2, P2) to end.
Rnd 3: K all.
Rnd 4: P all.
Rep Rnds 1–4 for pattern.

DIRECTIONS

Body

Using smaller, longer circular needles, CO 204 (228, 252, 276)(300, 324, 348, 372) sts. PM for BOR and join to work in the rnd, being careful not to twist sts.
Work 2x2 Rib until piece measures 1.5″ from CO edge.

Switch to larger circular needles and work Waffle Stitch pattern until piece measures 16.25 (16.5, 16.75, 17)(17.5, 18, 18.25, 18.25)″ from CO edge, or desired length to underarm, ending after Rnd 2 of pattern.
Next Rnd: K102 (114, 126, 138)(150, 162, 174, 186), PM for side, K to end.
Next Rnd: P to 2 (2, 2, 2)(4, 4, 4, 4) sts before M, BO 4 (4, 4, 4)(8, 8, 8, 8) sts removing M, P to 2 (2, 2, 2)(4, 4, 4, 4) sts before BOR, BO 4 (4, 4, 4)(8, 8, 8, 8) sts removing M. Place first 98 (110, 122, 134)(142, 154, 166, 178) sts on st holder or scrap yarn for front.

Back

Work in Waffle Stitch (worked flat) until back measures 6.75 (6.75, 7, 7.25)(7.75, 8, 8.25, 8.5)″ from underarm BO, ending after a WS row.
Next Row (RS): Work 38 (40, 42, 44)(46, 50, 56, 62) sts as established, BO 22 (30, 38, 46)(50, 54, 54, 54) sts, work as established to end. Place first 38 (40, 42, 44)(46, 50, 56, 62) sts on st holder or scrap yarn for Right Back Shoulder.

Left Back Shoulder

Row 1 (WS): Work as established to last 2 sts, P2tog TBL. 1 st dec.
Row 2 (RS): BO 2 sts, work as established to end. 2 sts dec.
Rows 3–4: Rep Rows 1–2. 32 (34, 36, 38)(40, 44, 50, 56) sts remain for shoulder.
Row 5: BO 8 (8, 9, 9)(10, 11, 12, 14) sts, work as established to end.
Row 6: WE as established.
Rows 7–8: Rep Rows 5–6.
Row 9: BO 8 (9, 9, 10)(10, 11, 13, 14) sts, work as established to end.
Row 10: WE as established.
BO all sts.

Right Back Shoulder

Join yarn to work a WS row.
Row 1 (WS): BO 2 sts, work as established to end. 2 sts dec.
Row 2 (RS): Work as established to last 2 sts, K2tog. 1 st dec.
Row 3: Rep Row 1.
Row 4: BO 8 (8, 9, 9)(10, 11, 12, 14) sts, work as established to last 2 sts, K2tog.
Row 5: WE as established.
Row 6: BO 8 (8, 9, 9)(10, 11, 12, 14) sts, work as established to end.
Row 7: WE as established.
Row 8: BO 8 (9, 9, 10)(10, 11, 13, 14) sts, work as established to end.
Row 9: WE as established.
BO all remaining sts.

Front

Join yarn to work a WS row. Work Waffle Stitch pattern flat until piece measures 4.25 (4.25, 4.5, 5)(5.25, 5.5, 5.75, 6)″ from underarm BO, ending after a WS row.
Next Row (RS): Work 43 (45, 47, 49)(51, 55, 61, 67) sts as established, BO 12 (20, 28, 36)(40, 44, 44, 44) sts, work as established to end. Place first 43 (45, 47, 49)(51, 55, 61, 67) sts on st holder or scrap yarn for Left Front.

Right Front

Row 1 (WS): Work as established to last 2 sts, P2tog TBL. 1 st dec.
Row 2 (RS): BO 2 sts, work as established to end. 2 sts dec.
Rows 3–4: Rep Rows 1–2. 37 (39, 41, 43)(45, 49, 55, 61) sts.
Row 5: WE as established.

Dec Row (RS): K1, SSK, work as established to end. 1 st dec.
Next Row (WS): WE as established.
Rep Dec Row every RS row two more times, then every fourth row two times. 32 (34, 36, 38)(40, 44, 50, 56) sts remain for shoulder.
WE until armhole measures 7.25 (7.25, 7.5, 8)(8.25, 8.5, 8.75, 9)″ from underarm BO, ending after a RS row.
Next Row (WS): BO 8 (8, 9, 9)(10, 11, 12, 14) sts, work as established to end.

Next Row (RS): WE as established.
Rep last two rows once more.
Next Row: BO 8 (9, 9, 10)(10, 11, 13, 14) sts, work as established to end.
Next Row: WE as established.
BO all sts.

Left Front
Join yarn to work a WS row.
Row 1 (WS): BO 2 sts, work as established to end.
Row 2 (RS): Work as established to last 2 sts, K2tog.
Rows 3–4: Rep Rows 1–2.
Row 5: WE as established.

Dec Row: Work as established to last 3 sts, K2tog, K1.
Rep Dec Row every RS row two mores times, then every fourth row two more times. 32 (34, 36, 38)(40, 44, 50, 56) sts remain for shoulder.
WE until armhole measures 7.25 (7.25, 7.5, 8)(8.25, 8.5, 8.75, 9)" from underarm BO, ending after a WS row.
Next Row (RS): BO 8 (8, 9, 9)(10, 11, 12, 14) sts, work as established to end.
Next Row (WS): WE established.
Rep last two rows once more.
Next Row: BO 8 (9, 9, 10)(10, 11, 13, 14) sts, work as established to end.
Next Row: WE as established.
BO all sts.

Seam shoulders tog.

Sleeves (make two the same)
Note: Switch to larger DPNs when there are too few sts to work comfortably on circular needles.
With larger, shorter circular needles, beginning at center of underarm BO, PU and K: 2 (2, 2, 2)(4, 4, 4, 4) sts in underarm, 38 (40, 42, 44)(44, 46, 48, 48) sts up to shoulder seam (approx 2 sts for every three rows), 38 (40, 42, 44)(44, 46, 48, 48) sts down to underarm (approx 2 sts for every three rows), 2 (2, 2, 2)(4, 4, 4, 4) sts in underarm. 80 (84, 88, 92)(96, 100, 104, 104) sts. PM for BOR.
Work Rnds 1–4 of Waffle Stitch pattern in the rnd.

Dec Rnd: K1, SSK, work as established to last 3 sts, K2tog, K1. 2 sts dec.
Cont working as established and rep Dec Rnd every 7 (6, 6, 6)(5, 5, 5, 5) rnds 17 (19, 21, 21)(23, 23, 25, 25) more times. 44 (44, 44, 48)(48, 48, 52, 52) sts remaining.
WE, if necessary, until sleeve measures 17" or 1" shorter than desired length.
Switch to smaller DPNs. Work 2x2 Rib for 1".
BO in pattern.

Finishing
Weave in ends, wash, and block to diagram.

Neckband
With smaller, shorter circular needle, begin at right shoulder seam. With RS facing, PU and K: 2 sts for every three rows down to back neck BO, 1 st in every BO st, 2 sts for every three rows up to left shoulder seam, 2 sts for every three rows down to front neck BO, 1 st in each BO st, 2 sts for every three rows up to right shoulder seam. Exact st count is not important, but should be a multiple of 4. Adjust number of sts with incs or decs on first rnd if necessary.
Work 2x2 Rib for five rnds.
BO in pattern.

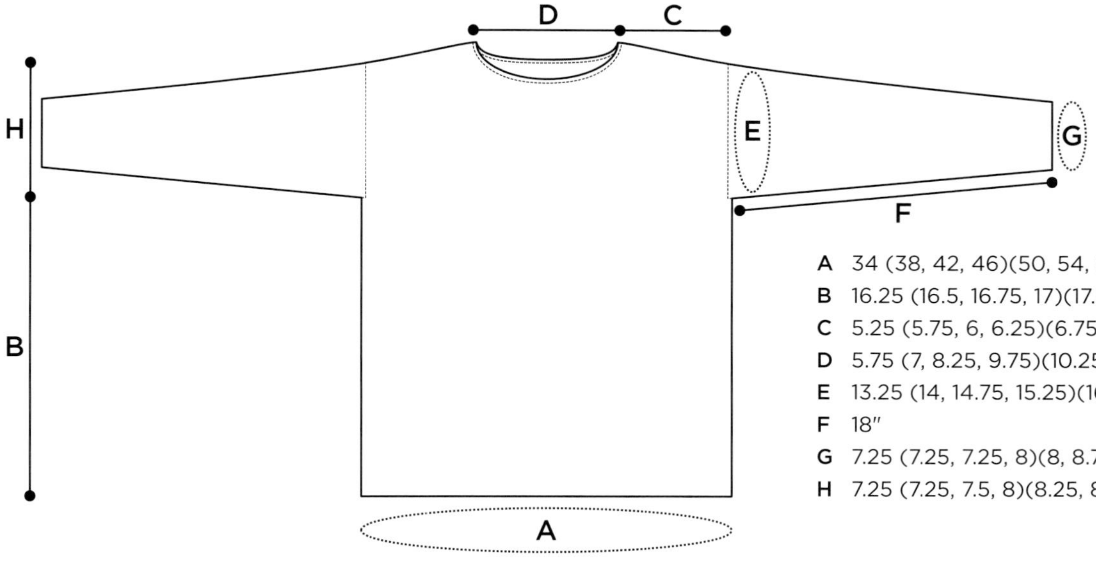

A 34 (38, 42, 46)(50, 54, 58, 62)"
B 16.25 (16.5, 16.75, 17)(17.5, 18, 18.25, 18.25)"
C 5.25 (5.75, 6, 6.25)(6.75, 7.25, 8.25, 9.25)"
D 5.75 (7, 8.25, 9.75)(10.25, 11, 11, 11)"
E 13.25 (14, 14.75, 15.25)(16, 16.75, 17.25, 17.25)"
F 18"
G 7.25 (7.25, 7.25, 8)(8, 8.75, 8.75, 8.75)"
H 7.25 (7.25, 7.5, 8)(8.25, 8.5, 8.75, 9)"

CEDAR CREEK
GRIST MILL

Glossary

Common Stitches & Techniques

Slipped Stitches (Sl)
Always slip stitches purl-wise with yarn held to the wrong side of work, unless noted otherwise in the pattern.

Make 1 Left-Leaning Stitch (M1L)
Inserting LH needle from front to back, PU the horizontal strand between the st just worked and the next st, and K TBL.

Make 1 Right-Leaning Stitch (M1R)
Inserting LH needle from back to front, PU the horizontal strand between the st just worked and the next st, and K TFL.

Slip, Slip, Knit (SSK)
(Sl1 K-wise) twice; insert LH needle into front of these 2 sts and knit them together.

Centered Double Decrease (CDD)
Slip first and second sts together as if to work K2tog; K1; pass 2 slipped sts over the knit st.

Stockinette Stitch (St st, flat over any number of sts)
Row 1 (RS): Knit all sts.
Row 2 (WS): Purl all sts.
Rep Rows 1-2 for pattern.
St st in the round: *Knit every rnd.*

Garter Stitch (in the round over any number of sts)
Rnd 1: Purl all sts.
Rnd 2: Knit all sts.
Rep Rnds 1-2 for pattern.
Garter Stitch flat: *Knit every row.*
(One Garter ridge is comprised of two rows/rnds.)

1x1 Rib (flat or in the round, over an even number of sts)
Row/Rnd 1: (K1, P1) to end of row/rnd.
Rep Row/Rnd 1 for pattern.

2x2 Rib (flat over a multiple of 4 sts plus 2)
Row 1 (RS): K2, (P2, K2) to end of row.
Row 2 (WS): P2, (K2, P2) to end of row.
Rep Rows 1-2 for pattern.

2x2 Rib (in the round over a multiple of 4 sts)
Rnd 1: (K2, P2) to end of rnd.
Rep Rnd 1 for pattern.

Knitting in the Round
The Magic Loop technique uses one long circular needle to knit around a small circumference. The Two Circulars technique uses two long circular needles to knit around a small circumference. Photo and video tutorials for these, plus using DPNs and 16″ circular needles, can be found at knitpicks.com/learning-center/knitting-in-round.

Backward Loop Cast On
A simple, all-purpose cast on that can be worked mid-row. Also called Loop, Single, or E-Wrap Cast On. A tutorial can be found at tutorials.knitpicks.com/loop-cast-on.

Long Tail Cast On
Fast and neat once you get the hang of it. Also referred to as the Slingshot Cast On. A tutorial can be found at knitpicks.com/learning-center/learn-to-knit.

Cabled Cast On
A strong and nice looking basic cast on that can be worked mid-project. A tutorial can be found at tutorials.knitpicks.com/cabled-cast-on.

Knitted Cast On
A basic cast on that can be worked mid-project. A tutorial can be found at tutorials.knitpicks.com/knitted-cast-on.

3-Needle Bind Off
Used to easily seam two rows of live stitches together. A tutorial can be found at knitpicks.com/learning-center/3-needle-bind-off.

Abbreviations

approx	approximately
BO	bind off
BOR	beginning of round
CN	cable needle
C (1, 2…)	color (1, 2…)
CC	contrast color
CDD	centered double decrease (*see above*)
CO	cast on
cont	continue
dec(s)	decrease(es)
DPN(s)	double pointed needle(s)
inc(s)	increase(s)
K	knit
K2tog	knit 2 stitches together
K3tog	knit 3 stitches together
KFB	knit into front and back of stitch
K-wise	knit-wise
LH	left hand
M	marker
M1	make 1 stitch
M1L	make 1 left-leaning stitch (*see above*)
M1R	make 1 right-leaning stitch (*see above*)
MC	main color
P	purl
P2tog	purl 2 stitches together
P3tog	purl 3 stitches together
PM	place marker
PFB	purl into front and back of stitch
PSSO	pass slipped stitch over
PU	pick up
P-wise	purl-wise
rep	repeat
Rev St st	reverse stockinette stitch
RH	right hand
rnd(s)	round(s)
RS	right side
Sk	skip
SK2P	slip 1, knit 2 together, pass slipped stitch over
SKP	slip, knit, pass slipped stitch over
Sl	slip (*see above*)
SM	slip marker
SSK	slip, slip, knit these 2 stitches together (*see above*)
SSP	slip, slip, purl these 2 stitches together through back loop
SSSK	slip, slip, slip, knit these 3 stitches together (like SSK)
St st	stockinette stitch (*see above*)
st(s)	stitch(es)
TBL	through back loop
TFL	through front loop
tog	together
W&T	wrap & turn (for short rows; *see next pg*)
WE	work even
WS	wrong side
WYIB	with yarn in back
WYIF	with yarn in front
YO	yarn over

Cables
Tutorials for different kinds of cables, including 1 over 1 and 2 over 2, with and without cable needles, can be found at knitpicks.com/learning-center/guides/cables.

Felted Join (to splice yarn)
One method for joining a new length of yarn to the end of one that is already being used. A tutorial can be found at tutorials.knitpicks.com/felted-join.

Mattress Stitch
A neat, invisible seaming method that uses the bars between the first and second stitches on the edges. A tutorial can be found at tutorials.knitpicks.com/mattress-stitch.

Provisional Cast On (crochet method)
Used to cast on stitches that are also a row of live stitches, so they can be put onto a needle and used later.
Directions: Using a crochet hook, make a slip knot, then hold knitting needle in left hand, hook in right. With yarn in back of needle, work a chain st by pulling yarn over needle and through chain st. Move yarn back to behind needle, and rep for the number of sts required. Chain a few more sts off the needle, then break yarn and pull end through last chain. (CO sts may be incorrectly mounted; if so, work into backs of these sts.) To unravel later (when sts need to be picked up), pull chain end out; chain should unravel, leaving live sts. A video tutorial can be found at tutorials.knitpicks.com /crocheted-provisional-cast-on.

Provisional Cast On (crochet chain method)
Same result as the crochet method above, but worked differently, so you may prefer one or the other.
Directions: With a crochet hook, use scrap yarn to make a slip knot and chain the number of sts to be cast on, plus a few extra sts. Insert tip of knitting needle into first bump of crochet chain. Wrap project yarn around needle as if to knit, and pull yarn through crochet chain, forming first st. Rep this process until you have cast on the correct number of sts. To unravel later (when sts need to be picked up), pull chain out, leaving live sts. A photo tutorial can be found at tutorials.knitpicks.com/crocheted-provisional-cast-on.

Judy's Magic Cast On
This method creates stitches coming out in opposite directions from a seamless center line, perfect for starting toe-up socks.
Directions: Make a slip knot and place loop around one of the two needles; anchor loop counts as first st. Hold needles tog, with needle that yarn is attached to on top. In other hand, hold yarn so tail goes over index finger and yarn attached to ball goes over thumb. Bring tip of bottom needle over strand of yarn on finger (top strand), around and under yarn and back up, making a loop around needle. Pull loop snug. Bring top needle (with slip knot) over yarn tail on thumb (bottom strand), around and under yarn and back up, making a loop around needle. Pull loop snug. Cont casting on sts until desired number is reached; top yarn strand always wraps around bottom needle, and bottom yarn strand always wraps around top needle. A tutorial can be found at tutorials.knitpicks.com/judys-magic-cast-on.

Stretchy Bind Off
Directions: K2, *insert LH needle into front of 2 sts on RH needle and knit them tog—1 st remains on RH needle. K1; rep from * until all sts have been bound off. A tutorial can be found at tutorials.knitpicks.com/go-your-own-way-socks-toe-up-part-7-binding-off.

Jeny's Surprisingly Stretchy Bind Off (for 1x1 Rib)
Directions: Reverse YO, K1, pass YO over; *YO, P1, pass YO and previous st over P1; reverse YO, K1, pass YO and previous st over K1; rep from * until 1 st is left, then break working yarn and pull it through final st to complete BO.

Kitchener Stitch (also called Grafting)
Seamlessly join two sets of live stitches together.
Directions: With an equal number of sts on two needles, break yarn leaving a tail approx four times as long as the row of sts, and thread through a blunt yarn needle. Hold needles parallel with WSs facing in and both needles pointing to the right. Perform Step 2 on the first front st, then Step 4 on the first back st, then continue from Step 1, always pulling yarn tightly so the grafted row tension matches the knitted fabric:
Step 1: Pull yarn needle K-wise through front st and drop st from knitting needle.
Step 2: Pull yarn needle P-wise through next front st, leaving st on knitting needle.
Step 3: Pull yarn needle P-wise through first back st and drop st from knitting needle.
Step 4: Pull yarn needle K-wise through next back st, leaving st on knitting needle.
Rep Steps 1-4 until all sts have been grafted together, finishing by working Step 1 through the last remaining front st, then Step 3 through the last remaining back st. Photo tutorials can be found at knitpicks.com/learning-center/learn-to-knit/kitchener.

Short Rows
There are several options for how to handle short rows, so you may see different suggestions/intructions in a pattern.

Wrap and Turn (W&T) (one option for Short Rows)
Work until the st to be wrapped. If knitting: Bring yarn to front, Sl next st P-wise, return yarn to back; turn work, and Sl wrapped st onto RH needle. Cont across row. If purling: Bring yarn to back of work, Sl next st P-wise, return yarn to front; turn work and Sl wrapped st onto RH needle. Cont across row.
Picking up Wraps: Work to wrapped st. If knitting: Insert RH needle under wrap, then through wrapped st K-wise; K st and wrap tog. If purling: Sl wrapped st P-wise onto RH needle, use LH needle to lift wrap and place it onto RH needle; Sl wrap and st back onto LH needle, and P tog.
A tutorial for W&T can be found at tutorials.knitpicks.com /short-rows-wrap-and-turn-or-wt.

German Short Rows (another option for Short Rows)
Work to turning point; turn. WYIF, Sl first st P-wise. Bring yarn over back of right needle, pulling firmly to create a "double stitch" on RH needle. If next st is a K st, leave yarn at back; if next st is a P st, bring yarn to front between needles. When it's time to work into double st, knit both strands tog.

THIS COLLECTION FEATURES

Knit Picks yarn is both luxe and affordable—a seeming contradiction trounced! But it's not just about the pretty colors; we also care deeply about fiber quality and fair labor practices, leaving you with a gorgeously reliable product you'll turn to time and time again.

View these beautiful
yarns and more at
www.KnitPicks.com